YORKSHIRE'S GINS

THE SPIRIT OF THE DALES, THE MOORS, CITIES & COAST

FIONA LAING

GREAT NORTHERN

Fiona Laing is the author of The GIN CLAN, the comprehensive guide to Scottish gin. She has been writing about food and drink for more than a decade and for this book on Yorkshire gin has returned to the county where she lived in her teens and has family connections. Her writing on drinks started when she worked with the first Indian single malt whisky to launch in Europe. Other spirits and wine were never far behind as she travelled the world, listening to the stories of the makers. Food editor, hotel judge, travel writer, Fiona has explored food and drink whenever her career as a newspaper journalist and PR consultant has allowed.

Great Northern Books Limited
PO Box 1380, Bradford, BD5 5FB
www.greatnorthernbooks.co.uk

ISBN: 978-1-912101-01-6

Design and layout: David Burrill

CIP Data
A catalogue for this book is available
from the British Library

CONTENTS

Yorkshire gin — 5

What's in a name? — 5

The taste of juniper — 6

Why Yorkshire? — 7

The gin drinkers — 10

Who makes it? — 10

The Distilling Clan — 13

The Kith & Kin — 85

Tonic water — 123

Author's thanks — 126

Index — 127

Sing Gin

YORKSHIRE GIN

Yorkshire is probably the most marketable county in England. It certainly has good reason: great food and drink, fertile and dramatic landscapes and people with grit, determination and pride. It all means God's Own County is a great place to make gin.

Makers have plenty of scope to use Yorkshire's hero ingredients: the gorse and heather from the moors, the sloes, elderflowers and hips from the hedgerows, the rhubarb, lavender, roses, herbs and honey … or traditional flavours like liquorice or ginger.

Yorkshire, of all England's counties, has plenty of history, folklore and traditions to call on when inspiring brands. And its industrial legacy provides skills and technical expertise to bring them to market.

It is not surprising then that there is a brigade of gin makers who are devising, distilling and selling imaginative and innovative gins right across the county.

WHAT'S IN A NAME?

But what makes a gin a "Yorkshire gin"? Is it using ingredients from the county? Or water from a Yorkshire spring? Is it making the base spirit from scratch on site? Does the juniper need to be picked in Yorkshire? Does the distiller need to be born and bred in one of the Ridings? Does the distillery have to be in Yorkshire?

The gin industry is not tightly tied up in rules and regulations, so there is no guidance on what might constitute Yorkshire gin. Where is the line to be drawn? Instinctively you might say a Yorkshire gin is one "made in Yorkshire", but that definition would rule out several gins you would expect to be in a book of Yorkshire gins.

To recognise the importance of "made in Yorkshire", I have used the classification I devised for The GIN CLAN, my book of Scottish gins and distilleries. Using Scottish terms, which I hope still ring bells in Yorkshire, the entries appear under the headings "The Clan" and "Kith & Kin".

The Distilling Clan are the distilleries – its members have a still in Yorkshire, and they use it to make gin.

The Kith & Kin are the rest: those we think of as Yorkshire gins. There are makers, creators and brand owners who have gin made for them in Yorkshire – and elsewhere. They could be makers who use compounding techniques to create "bathtub" gins. Some of the Kith & Kin plan on building their own distilleries, so will graduate to the Clan in due course.

The classification is not perfect, but it is a neat reflection of the Yorkshire gin family in 2020.

And to be clear, this is a book about gin – full-strength gin.

THE TASTE OF JUNIPER

In the European Union, the minimum bottled strength for "distilled gin" and "gin" is 37.5% ABV (alcohol by volume). This book concentrates on those gins. There are also "juniper-flavoured spirit drinks" – including Dutch jenever or genever – with their own rules and bottled at a minimum of 30% ABV. And many fruit liqueurs – some marketed as fruit gins – but below 37.5% ABV.

The EU defines "distilled gin" as one made by redistilling alcohol of agricultural origin with an initial strength of 96% ABV in stills traditionally used for gin in the presence of juniper berries and other natural botanicals. The juniper taste must be predominant. London gin and London Dry gin are types of distilled gin with nothing added after distillation apart from water.

Alongside that is "gin", a juniper-flavoured spirit drink produced by flavouring neutral alcohol of agricultural origin with juniper berries and other natural substances. Again the taste must predominantly be that of juniper. This category includes what is referred to as "compound" or "bathtub" gin.

In each definition, there is the stipulation for gin to have a "juniper-led" flavour.

As makers become more and more adventurous in their choice of botanicals, the juniper flavour can almost disappear, and, as many point out, if you leave out the juniper it is just a flavoured vodka. Compared to Scotch whisky, which has more than a century of tight regulation, gin has very light rules and plenty of scope for innovative interpretation. And many people are loath to dampen that spirit of creativity. The debate around juniper will continue.

Another area of concern is that you see the word "gin" used on products that are obviously not gin. There have even been non-alcoholic brands launched which make a play of being "not gin". And liqueurs can often make much of the gin part of their brand, although they contain very little gin and are bottled at well below 37.5% ABV.

All this might not matter to the consumer if they enjoy what they are drinking, but some makers are concerned about the potential damage to the reputation of their premium product.

WHY YORKSHIRE?

In recent years, consumers' priorities have been shifting; more people are interested in the details of the products they buy: where it comes from, what is in it, how it is made, and who makes it.

The focus is provenance, closely linked to sustainability. As you will see in this book, Yorkshire gin really chimes with those interests – the stories about the makers and their gin journeys reveal the details of the "where", "what", "how" and "who".

And Yorkshire has established a reputation for fine food and drink. Just look at the Michelin-star restaurants, artisan producers, farmers' markets and food festivals for evidence of the popularity of its produce and products.

Tom Naylor-Leyland has witnessed this growth in interest in Yorkshire flavours since establishing Malton's Food Lovers Festival in 2009. "Ten years later we had 40,000 visitors for the festival and up to 5,000 at our monthly food markets," he says, adding that encouraging artisans – including Rare Bird Gin – to make their produce in the town is key to its position as the "food capital" of Yorkshire.

In turn, Yorkshire has been called the food capital of England. Eddy Lascelles, managing director of the Harewood Food & Drink Project, explains its appeal: "Yorkshire is a huge diverse county with a deeply-rooted heritage around agriculture and horticulture practice and, of course, a long coastline. If you throw into the mix the big buzzing cities and urbanised areas like Leeds and Sheffield, they create a really exciting food and drink scene. It has both cutting-edge contemporary food and the slow food, agricultural element."

What is notable in the Yorkshire gin scene is how important hero botanicals are – and how many come from the area around a maker's home. However, the key gin ingredient – juniper – does not grow widely in Yorkshire and most makers import it, usually from eastern Europe.

Allied Glass

A favourite local ingredient in Yorkshire gin is rhubarb, but soft fruit, hedgerow berries, ginger and flax all feature.

Yorkshire forced rhubarb is one of the county's handful of products with a Protected Designation of Origin status. It means it must be grown in the dark in the area designated as the Rhubarb Triangle which lies between Leeds, Wakefield and Bradford.

The technique dates back to a chance discovery in 1817 that was put to commercial use by the ingenuity of farmers using forcing sheds in what is now the Triangle.

Janet Oldroyd, managing director of one of the best-known rhubarb-forcing farms, noticed the demand for bulk supplies growing from about 2012. Then, gin – and other drink – makers started buying direct, with Slingsby leading the way.

Another popular gin makers' ingredient is liquorice root. In truth, it is used in many gins for its natural sweetness and ability to change the texture of a gin. However, in Yorkshire it takes on added significance thanks to Pontefract cakes. The black circular sweets were developed in the 1760s by George Dunhill, an apothecary in the town, who added sugar to the root of the liquorice bush which thrived in the loamy, sandy soil of that part of Yorkshire.

His invention ensured a thriving industry in the town for almost 200 years. Although liquorice is no longer the force it once was for Pontefract – and the fields long since dug up – a recent resurgence of interest in it has prompted farmers Heather and Rob Copley to plant new fields of liquorice.

Farmed lavender and seaweed are among the other produce cultivated in Yorkshire that gin makers have been able to turn to when foraging in the wild is not sustainable.

No gin is complete without water, and that is something Yorkshire has in abundance. Makers use it to dilute the spirit that comes from the still, and they have some of the best water to work with.

Whether it is from the Pennines, the Wolds or the Harrogate aquifer, each source has its own unique attributes and distillers will carefully develop their recipes so that the water enhances the gin perfectly.

The makers are also supported by Yorkshire suppliers of the practical things they need to take their gin into the market. There are talented artists and graphic designers, bottle engravers and packaging suppliers to call on.

On the production side, Yorkshire's manufacturing heritage comes into its own. Karmelle of Huddersfield is a leader in the design and manufacture of liquid filling, capping and labelling machines for the food and drink industry, while Allied Glass makes bottles at its sites to the south of Leeds.

"We've seen a big increase in the demand from craft distillers over the past three to four years, and they are looking for flair and creativity," says Phil Morris, a director of Allied Glass, which was founded in the late 1800s and still operates from its original sites.

"They want to come to someone who can supply not only the glass, but also added-value decorations – like colour coating or designs printed directly on the bottles. There are that many gins available that people want to have their products stand out."

Among Allied's bespoke gin containers are the clever Yorkshire Rose base of Masons' bottles, the tactile embossing for Sir Robin of Locksley and the intricate direct printing for the Folklore Society.

THE GIN DRINKERS

Making gin and putting it into bottles is never going to be a success without the consumers … and getting a maker's message out to the marketplace is rarely done without help.

The retailers and bar staff which promote Yorkshire's gins are an important part of the picture. The Evil Eye in York with its record-breaking gin stock is just one of many places drawing attention to Yorkshire's gin and selling bottles of it. And what town doesn't now have a gin bar – or at least a pub which promotes local gins?

Then, there are restaurants and hotels who are working with makers to create their own house gins. Not all collaborations are as ambitious as the link-up between Slingsby and Michael O'Hare, the chef-patron of the Michelin-starred Man Behind the Curtain in Leeds, which used caviar in their gin.

Yorkshire distillers are also making the most of talking directly to the public. The gin experience comes in different forms – from distillery tours and gin schools to tastings and festivals.

Two influential UK-wide gin festival organisers are based in Yorkshire. The Gin Lounge founded by Amanda Ludlow operates from York, while Earles & Co, the Leeds-based organiser of the Gin Fayres, was founded by Jasmine Wheelhouse.

Meeting a gin's distiller is one of the joys of exploring the gin world. We are often lucky enough to meet them at festivals as we "taste before we buy". Some welcome visitors to their distilleries and share their secrets – a few will even help you make your own gin. The number of distilleries with gin experiences means it could be the basis for a very pleasant itinerary for anyone wanting to make a holiday in Yorkshire.

WHO MAKES IT?

Gin might have largely gone out of fashion in the 20th century, but James Bond and Gordon's kept it in the public consciousness. People became more interested in gin again as they found Bombay Sapphire in the 1990s and, when the premium gins such as Hendrick's and Tanqueray No. Ten were launched as the new century dawned, there was a renewed appetite for the old favourite, especially in cocktails. When legislation changed and allowed smaller stills, the artisan or craft gin makers stepped up, led by Sipsmith, the architect of the rule change. At the end of this century's first decade, whisky makers were also testing the water. The Botanist, Caorunn and Edinburgh Gin came from companies with established whisky brands.

The first gin from Yorkshire appeared in 2013 when Masons launched. The following year Locksley debuted and six more came to market the year after. In 2020, the Yorkshire gin family spans more than 60 brands.

The makers are from all walks of life: from farming and hospitality to the military and marketing – there is no pigeon-holing a gin maker. Reasons to make gin are as numerous as the entries in this book. The dreams of the makers are what fuels much of the modern gin boom.

There are the farmers looking to diversify their livelihood, the entrepreneurs wanting to celebrate their beautiful hometown and the gin enthusiasts who wanted to have a go themselves. There are some solely focused on gin, a number who are producing gin as a step to making whisky and those who are making it alongside beer and other drinks, including tonics. For some, making gin is the purely commercial addition of a brand to a portfolio of drinks.

Whatever the reason, it all adds up to the overall picture of gin selling like the proverbial hot cakes.

Wine & Spirits Trade Association figures show that sales in the UK in the 12 months to June 2019 were valued at £2.5 billion. The continued popularity of gin helped push the total to more than 80 million bottles.

A trend which has been noted is the growth in the popularity of pink and flavoured gin. Data for 2018 showed that flavoured gin had driven more than half the growth in gin, despite only making up one-fifth of total sales. And almost three-quarters of flavoured gin's contribution to that growth has been driven by pink gin.

Will pink gins continue to attract the attention? Some say the next trend will be savoury flavours, others point to the next "big thing" being flavoured rum … or perhaps absinthe or mezcal.

For now, let's raise a glass and toast Yorkshire's gin makers.

THE
DISTILLING CLAN

Clan (a tribe or collection of families subject to a single chieftain, commonly bearing the same surname and supposed to have a common ancestor)

These are the gin distillers of Yorkshire. They have a physical still in Yorkshire where they make gin. They may also make other spirits – there are several whisky distilleries, as well as makers of rum, absinthe, vodka and liqueurs. In some cases, they make gin for other brand owners under contract, or they may allow "cuckoo" distillers to use their stills to make gin.

The distilleries are listed by their name or company's name – not necessarily the name of the gin.

CAPTAIN COOK DISTILLERY
[Navigator: First Voyage]

Stokesley, North Yorkshire
captaincookdistillery.co.uk
First gin: April 2018

Yorkshireman, Captain James Cook was brought up at Great Ayton near Stokesley, and then went to work in a shop at Staithes on the coast before becoming a merchant navy apprentice with a small fleet based in Whitby.

Having joined the Royal Navy in 1755, Cook worked his way up through the ranks before he was offered his first command in 1768. It was for a scientific expedition to the Pacific, and his ship, HMS Endeavour, was built by Thomas Fishburn in Whitby.

It was on that journey in April 1770 that Cook's crew first set foot on the Australian continent at what he named Botany Bay.

As the 250th anniversary of the start of Cook's voyage approached, a distillery was being born in Stokesley. Its name celebrated the market town's famous son and its first gin was named Navigator: First Voyage in honour of his epic journey.

The North Yorkshire Dry gin uses ten botanicals, including juniper, coriander, angelica root, orange and lemon peels and heather tips from the nearby North York Moors.

The distillery was created by John Toovey who, when he retired as a sales director for an international chemicals company, had set up Wainstones Brewery in Stokesley in 2010. He also ran the Captain Cook Brewery. When the brewing operations moved to Hutton Rudby, there was an empty unit available and the idea of a microdistillery was born.

The former Wainstones Brewery was converted into a distillery with a 100-litre traditional copper pot alembic still, named Emily, installed. For recipe trials Little Emily, a 5-litre sister pot still, is put into use.

Ross Buchanan, a brewer turned distiller, is in day-to-day charge of the distillery. Having studied distilling at Brewlab in Sunderland, the experienced brewer spent three months honing the London Dry recipe for Navigator.

He has since made another two gins – Rhubarb and Honey & Citrus – and a double-distilled vodka was launched in the autumn of 2019.

COOPER KING DISTILLERY
[Cooper King Dry Gin, Herb Gin]

Sutton-on-the-Forest,
North Yorkshire
www.cooperkingdistillery.co.uk
First gin: May 2018

For Abbie Neilson and Chris Jaume their dream was to distil an English whisky underpinned by craftsmanship, honesty and adventure. The dream had taken shape on a backpacking adventure in the Southern Hemisphere.

In Tasmania, they had fallen in love with the island's whisky which was taking the malt world by storm. During their stay there, they studied Tasmanian whisky making and toured distilleries, learning as much as they could.

As they continued their travels, Abbie, a biomedical scientist, and Chris, a chartered architect, formulated their plan to self-build a craft distillery at home in Yorkshire.

In 2016, they embarked on turning a former stable on family land into a sustainable spirits business, installing a 900-litre Tasmanian copper pot still named Neilson after Abbie's father, and creating a warehouse, tasting room and shop.

With the support of members of their founders' club, family and grants, by June 2019 it was ready for production and they made their first malt whisky. They are now waiting for it to mature in 2023.

Of course, a distillery can make other spirits, so Abbie and Chris first launched a gin, using state-of-the-art vacuum distillation techniques on Büchi rotary evaporators with 5-litre glass flasks.

Cooper King Dry Gin uses 12 botanicals including Yorkshire lavender and cardamom for savoury and floral notes, plus honey from their own beehives. By using rich malt spirit and smooth wheat spirit, the Cooper King gins are smooth enough to be enjoyed neat or with ice.

Herb Gin, which combines fresh basil, lemongrass and clove, followed, adding a fresh herbaceous gin to the line-up.

Abbie, who is responsible for the distilling process, has also released small-batch, experimental spirits. The Pilot Series includes Black Cardamom botanical vodka, Berry + Basil liqueur and a new-make spirit,

the precursor of the whisky. A collaboration with That Boutique-y Gin Company resulted in Summertide Gin and a gin has been developed with chef Neil Bentinck for his York restaurant Skosh. Other gin collaborations are sure to follow.

The distillery's name is from Chris's great-great-grandfather, Charles Cooper King, an adventurer, who in 1885 documented the family history, dating his earliest ancestors – the Pigot (or Pygott) of Yorkshire – to 1030. A reference to a barrel-maker, meant Cooper King fitted perfectly. The shield in the distillery's logo reflects the family coat of arms.

Chris and Abbie's sustainable approach to creating the distillery has not only involved the use of renewable energy, planting trees to offset carbon dioxide, keeping their own bees and offering a bottle refill service, but has also incorporated the talents of local craftspeople.

Emily Stubbs, the artist and ceramicist responsible for artwork on the gin bottles is based in York, while Quentin Jaume, the cabinetmaker who made the oak tables for the tasting room, is Chris's father. Harriet Pace, a York Minster stonemason, created the distillery entrance signs, using 18th-century stones from the Minster.

FORGED IN WAKEFIELD
[Forged in Wakefield Gins]

Wakefield, West Yorkshire
www.forgedinwakefield.com
First gin: December 2018

More makers than you would imagine have discovered that using their own name for their own brand is not always possible.

In Wakefield, Gary and Victoria Ford were not put off when they were challenged over the use of their name, Ford; instead they are using a strong alternative – Forged in Wakefield – and it says a lot about their journey from gin dream to reality.

Four years before their first gin was launched, they were engrossed in

making home brews and wines, foraging wild berries to use in their creations and merely dreaming of making spirits. Then, with a passion for gin, they decided to rise to the challenge and create one worthy of their name.

The process took about 18 months – navigating the red tape, buying the equipment, setting up the distillery in their garage and, of course, creating that gin. And it was all done hand in hand with their day jobs: Gary works in IT, Victoria is a hospital nurse and their daughter Olivia also helps out.

Based on a traditional recipe, their Original Gin is designed around their own tastes and so quite spicy. They macerate juniper and coriander seeds before a one-shot distillation to make sure all eight botanicals shine through in the gin which is bottled at 43% ABV.

Cherry Blossom Gin made its debut at the same time and introduces sweet cherry and buttery almond flavours to the Original by reducing the quantity of botanicals to make way for the fruit.

Other fruit editions have followed: Rhubarb & Ginger, Passion Fruit, Sherbet Lemon, Strawberry & Cinnamon and Spice Orange. Each recipe is carefully crafted on a still, which has a copper column made by a fabricator to Gary's own specification, and a stainless-steel boiler from

StillDragon. Using the finest organic ingredients they can source – and no added sugar or artificial additives – the Fords let the process take its time so that they get the purest gin possible.

In the autumn of 2019, Gary and Victoria launched the Yorkshire Strength 57% ABV edition. The Original's botanicals have been tailored to mellow the Navy Strength punch. Lemon balm and elderflower add a calming effect on the palate, while additional orange peel intensifies the citrus notes.

The bottles are dressed in labels which evoke the Art Deco feel of the Great Gatsby era and are designed by Luka Andjelkovic.

HARRISON DISTILLERY
[Royal Fox Gin]

Huddersfield, West Yorkshire
www.royalfoxgin.com
First gin: December 2018

Was using your own wedding as a blind tasting a bit sly? Or perfectly fitting behaviour for a gin called Fox?

The groom, Simon Harrison, had begun making gin as a hobby a couple of years before, and when he and his bride Laura started to plan their big day, they decided to use it as favours for their own wedding.

Having quickly fallen in love with distilling, Simon learned all he could about the craft and applied for his distiller's licence, thinking it might make a business at some point in the future. But fate intervened: he was made redundant and on the same day his HMRC licences arrived.

So, on the day he left his job as an operations manager in the recycling industry Simon launched Harrison Distillery at his home in a village south-east of Huddersfield.

A few weeks later his wedding guests gave the gin the thumbs-up and he was both married and in business.

The gin is made in Bertha, a traditional 40-litre copper pot still from Portugal. The recipe was developed in Annie, a 2.5-litre still, and all the bottling, sealing and labelling is done by hand – mostly by Simon, as Laura works as a nurse.

The couple came up with the idea of using a fox as their brand because they wanted an animal that would allow a design that incorporates a traditional alembic still. The image was created by commercial artist Dave Bull in Leeds, and the graphic design for the packaging is by Tracey Stead of Sable Creative of Sheffield.

The gin was originally named Crafty Fox as it is handcrafted, but it has since become the more elegant Royal Fox.

The signature Royal Fox London Dry-style gin has 11 botanicals including juniper, coriander, orris root, black and pink peppercorns, rosemary, bay leaf, rose hip, lime and orange peels. By using only the pure heart of the spirit from the still, Simon ensures the gin is exceptionally smooth.

It was followed by Forest Fruits Gin, which is ruby red and bursting with berries. The strawberry, raspberry, blackberry, blackcurrant and sweet black cherry are infused into a gin adapted from the original Royal Fox recipe. An Old Tom uses Yorkshire honey for a classic, sweeter-style gin.

To mark Royal Fox's new identity, Simon created a Navy Strength edition of his signature gin. Adding angelica root and adjusting the proportions of the botanicals allows the peppercorns to come through for a warm mouthfeel, making it a gin that is also great for sipping.

HARROGATE TIPPLE
[Harrogate Premium Gin]

Ripley, North Yorkshire
www.harrogatetipple.com
First gin: October 2016

Harrogate can be a seductive place. It captured the hearts of Steven and Sally Green on a short visit from London. Then, when they had moved their family to the spa town, it was the sight of a Harrogate product in a hotel in Moscow that gave Steve the idea of creating a Harrogate gin using the town's famous spring water.

Steve, a film and TV cameraman, and Sally a TV producer, set about turning their script into reality. As they were fans of an occasional "tipple", the title was obvious.

They linked up with one of the gin world's most experienced distillers, Tom Nichol, who was Tanqueray's master distiller for nearly a decade during his 42 years at Diageo before retiring and helping to create several craft gins.

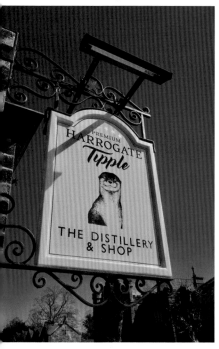

With Tom as a partner in the business, they created Harrogate Premium Gin, which features juniper, angelica root, orange peel, liquorice, lavender, pink grapefruit and coriander for a clean crisp balance of earthiness and fresh zest with a light lavender note. The gin is diluted to 43% ABV with Harrogate Spring Water.

Launched at the Royal Horticultural Society's botanical gardens at Harlow Carr in Harrogate where some of the botanicals had come from, the gin was made in Scotland. It met with a great response, so the next step was to make the gin themselves.

The initial idea of converting a town-centre smokehouse into a distillery was ultimately replaced by creating one on Ripley Castle estate, the home of Sir

Thomas Ingleby, four miles north of Harrogate. The estate has extensive walled gardens where they can now harvest some of their botanicals.

They moved into the distillery in January 2019, installing two 250-litre copper stills specially commissioned to Tom's specifications and named Cassie and Zak after two of the Greens' children.

The stills – which now make all their gin and rum – are under the supervision of Andrea Natiello, an Italian who had worked in the UK drinks industry before joining Harrogate Tipple and being tutored in distilling techniques by Tom.

Making up the Harrogate Gin cast are a pair of fruity gins. Gooseberry is made with fruit from Yorkshire and garden sorrel roots, while cornflower petals give the Blueberry edition its subtle blue colour.

The gins are all presented in chunky glass bottles adorned with the Harrogate Tipple mascot, Donnie the otter, which is named after the youngest member of the Green family. It was drawn by Mila Bailey an artist from South Africa who was 15 at the time. The Greens love the cheeky creatures which live in the rivers around Harrogate and thought they should have a starring role in their brand.

Harrogate Tipple, which also makes a rum and Downton Abbey Gin, opened a shop at the distillery in the summer of 2019. Visitors will be able to learn more about gin-making at the gin school which opens in 2020.

HAWORTH STEAM BREWING COMPANY
[Haworth Lamplighter, Deckchair, Spitfire, Miss Mollies]

West Yorkshire
haworthsteambrewery.co.uk
First gin: March 2017

Andy Gascoigne has shown time and again that keeping ahead of the game is the secret to successful entrepreneurship. He's already turned two remote pubs into must-visit destinations, set up popular microbreweries and is now producing not just gin but tonic as well.

The former rugby league player started this journey at the Waggon & Horses in Oxenhope, before heading to the Isle of Seil off the West Coast of Scotland. In both cases, he established microbreweries beside the pubs he took on.

It's not surprising then that when he, his wife Mandy and daughter Kelly moved back to their native Yorkshire, they took on another bar and promptly added a brewery.

This time it was in the picture-postcard Pennine village of Haworth, home of the Brontë sisters. In 2010, they opened the Haworth Steam Brewery and Bistro high up the cobbled Main Street of the thriving tourist destination.

Andy soon realised that interest in gin was starting to grow and decided to create his own spirits to showcase Yorkshire's heritage.

He went on a distilling course and used his long expertise in brewing to set up his distillery, installing a column still, Little Zak. It is named after an old family border collie and produces about 30 litres at a time.

First came Lamplighter, a handcrafted Dry gin using vapour-infused botanicals for a distinctive flavour with a clean, smooth finish. The botanicals are juniper, cassia bark, coriander, lemon peel, angelica, liquorice root and cardamom and it is bottled at 38% ABV.

Standing alongside this were the summery strawberry-infused Deckchair Gin and Yorkshire Rhubarb Gin, using forced rhubarb from the Yorkshire Triangle.

Then there is the limited edition "airforce strength" 45% ABV Spitfire Gin produced once a year to celebrate Haworth's 1940s weekend with proceeds going to SSAFA, the forces charity. It is based on the Lamplighter recipe but replaces cardamom with vanilla, almond and black pepper.

Miss Mollies is a series of sweetie-inspired gins. Think of the flavours of your childhood: Cherry Bon Bon, Old English Toffee, Pear Drops, Sherbet Lemon, Black Jack and Parma Violet. The gins are made by compounding Haworth's Lamplighter gin with the different flavours and bottled at 37.5% ABV.

In 2018, Andy added small-batch tonics and mixers to his range of Yorkshire-made products, selling them under his own name. An instant hit, he has installed specialist bottling and labelling lines to cope with demand.

With another successful business to his name, Andy is preparing for a new chapter and he expects to consolidate all his operations at a new location in 2020.

Then, he might be in a position to tackle the ultimate challenge of becoming a grain-to-glass distillery by using the brewery's wash to make base spirit for his own gins. It's a game plan worth watching.

HOOTING OWL DISTILLERY
[Hooting Owl Gins, VIE Spirited Gins]

Barmby Moor, East Yorkshire
hootingowldistillery.co.uk
First gin: September 2018

Inspiration comes from all sorts of places – and it's used in many ways. At Barmby Moor House, a carved stone owl prompted the name of its distillery, while the characteristics of the different parts of Yorkshire inspired the botanicals for its gins.

Making best use of this inspiration is Hooting Owl's founder and distiller Dominic M'Benga. An entrepreneur who has worked in the food services, green energy and defence industries, Dominic has restored the former coaching inn on the main York to Hull road and set up the distillery in its old stables.

There are seven stills: the first 60-litre still is known as Molly and its 30-litre sisters are June, Heather, Rosemary and Saffron. Two more 60-litre stills – Anne and Irene – arrived in the autumn of 2019.

The owl that sits over the entrance to the house has been developed into the distinctive character that embodies the Hooting Owl brand. The social media community has since named the owl Sir Owlfred Tyton-Hodging.

When it came to the gin, Dominic looked around him in Yorkshire and created a traditional London Dry-style with 16 botanicals as his signature gin. From the village history books, the 19th-century vicar of Barmby Moor who was posted to Mountain Ash in Wales prompted the inclusion of mountain ash.

Four more London Dry-style gins reflect the geographical areas of Yorkshire.

East Yorkshire Gin takes its botanical inspiration from a journey from sea and the rugged coast with kelp and through the Yorkshire Wolds with honey and hawthorn blossom and berries.

Heather and bilberries harvested on the Moors between Thirsk and

Whitby shine among the 19 botanicals of the North Yorkshire edition for a fruity gin.

South Yorkshire Gin is herby, with 18 botanicals including rosemary and mint inspired by the Barnsley Chop, a double loin cut of lamb.

West Yorkshire Gin comes from a more personal experience. Inspired by Dominic's hometown of Bradford,

it uses the traditional curry spices of cardamom, turmeric and cumin, sweetened by cassia bark and liquorice (which recalls Pontefract cakes).

Lining up alongside these gins is Veterans Strength, which is aged for three months before being bottled at 48% ABV.

In 2019, Dominic responded to calls to work his magic around the trend for fruit gins. Keen to stay true to his ethos of doing things differently, the VIE gins are sugar-free and natural. They are made from a smooth London Dry gin, which is then compounded with fruit flavours that have also been distilled in house to produce a concentrate. The VIE varieties include Yorkshire Raspberry, Parma Violet, Spiced Blood Orange and Rhubarb & Vanilla.

Hooting Owl also offers a contract distilling service for brand owners and already makes gins for the Evil Eye shop and cocktail bar in York and Artful Pour. More are due to appear for Quirky Ales in Leeds and the Pipe & Glass, a Michelin-starred pub and restaurant in South Dalton, near Beverley.

HOTHAM'S DISTILLERY
[Hotham's Handcrafted Gin, Cardamom Gin, Viola Old Tom, Pride in Hull]

Hull, East Yorkshire
www.hothams.co.uk
First gin: April 2018

Hull's maritime history has shaped the city on the Humber estuary. From the medieval monks who exported wool, through generations of merchants and fishermen, it has been a gateway for Yorkshire to the rest of the world.

In 1642, the military port and its large arsenal was a prize for King Charles I, and it was Sir John Hotham, the Governor of Hull, who denied the king access to the town. This defiance was the first "overt act" in the English Civil War and ultimately cost Sir John his life.

When Emma Kinton and Simon Pownall wanted a name for their distillery and gin school, it was to Sir John they turned.

They had themselves been to a gin school on one of their first dates and they loved the creative process so much that they bought and licensed a baby still to use at home.

Emma, a former teacher, and Simon, who had worked in IT and the newspaper industry, created a pair of gins, and, after receiving good feedback, they decided to set up a business around them.

They launched the two gins – Hotham's Handcrafted and Hotham's Cardamom – at the same time and then opened a gin school.

The signature gin has juniper berries, coriander seeds, gentian and orris roots, green cardamom pods, lavender and rose petals for a blend of spice, floral and earthy notes.

Cardamom Gin was developed by Simon after he was diagnosed with numerous allergies that meant he could no longer enjoy beer. He wanted to create a gin which would go as well with spicy foods as beer does.

Their distillery is in a shopping arcade in the Old Town and is tiny, with the gin made on small stills in micro-batches that are never more than 50 bottles. Bottling and labelling are done by hand.

The 40-litre copper alembic still is called Viola, named after a Humber-built steam trawler that served in the First World War, later became a whaling ship and is now laid up at the other side of the world in South Georgia.

Hotham's Viola Old Tom and London Dry gins support the Viola Trust, which is raising funds to bring the trawler back to Hull.

Limited editions from the distillery include Pride in Hull Gin, a Cardamom & Orange botanical vodka and a bespoke gin for 1884 Wine & Tapas Bar at Hull Marina.

Not content with one gin school, Emma and Simon opened a second in Leeds at the end of 2019 and a kombucha bar and bottle shop in Hull's Trinity Market. Kombucha is a lightly sparkling, green tea-based non-alcoholic drink which pairs well with gin.

HUMBER STREET DISTILLERY CO
[Hull Dry Gin, Trawler Gin]

Hull, East Yorkshire
hsdc.co.uk
First gin: May 2018

Like many waterside cities in the past, Hull had thriving market places where produce landed off the ships was traded. By the 19th century, the Fruit Market was one of its most important, with fresh produce bought and sold right beside the docks.

It is now the heart of a major urban regeneration project, transforming an area which was largely derelict just a few years ago into a thriving commercial, creative and residential community. At its heart is Humber Street where independent traders have colonised the old buildings.

The Humber Street Distillery serves more than 140 varieties of gin as well as an extensive line-up of spirits and craft beers and more cocktails than you can imagine.

Not content with adding a stylish gin bar to their hospitality portfolio, Lee Kirman and Charlotte Bailey wanted to create a distillery and make their own gin.

They enlisted the expertise of Jamie Baxter, the distiller who set up the City of London Distillery and created Chase Vodka and Burleigh's Gin, and learnt about making gin.

They installed an Arnold Holstein 150-litre copper pot still named

Lola Grace behind a glass wall in the bar. And, with their new-found knowledge, they created a citrus-led Hull Dry Gin which features cubeb berries, cassia bark, chamomile flowers, elderflower and pink grapefruit peel. The bottle sports Hull landmarks drawn by East Yorkshire-based architectural illustrator Nick Coupland.

In the summer of 2019, they launched Trawler Gin to support the Hull: Yorkshire's Maritime City restoration project. With a hint of samphire, the 13-botanical gin is bottled at 57% ABV in honour of the harsh and sometimes dangerous lives of the city's trawlermen.

There was also a testimonial gin for Danny Washbrook, the Hull FC rugby league player. Other limited editions have included Winter Gin, which added warming cinnamon, cloves and aromatic orange to the Humber Street Dry Gin recipe, while a Berry edition infused summer fruits with it.

Charlotte has been sharing the distillery's secrets with Matthew McDougall who is now looking after the gin-making. They work together on ideas for new editions and have rhubarb in their sights for a project. They have also made a four-times distilled vodka and are looking at collaborations with a brewery.

JACQSON
[JacqSon Yorkshire Dry Gin]

Netherton, near Huddersfield,
West Yorkshire
www.jacqson.co.uk
First gin: February 2017

Flavour is the key for Jacqueline Dumigan, founder of JacqSon. Not only is she an advocate of genuine juniper-led gin, but also the techniques she uses mean her botanicals bring their full flavour to her gins.

Jacqueline uses a rotary evaporator for vacuum distillation, which means a reduced boiling point for the alcohol so that it evaporates at a much lower temperature than in a traditional still.

That lower temperature is gentler on the botanicals and allows a greater intensity of their flavours and aromas to be retained.

Using small-batch vacuum distillation unleashed Jacqueline's imagination as she started to create gins to celebrate her part of Yorkshire.

With the Wakefield Triangle close at hand, rhubarb was a must for her first gin and when she realised liquorice was also grown locally they became the perfect partners in her signature JacqSon Gin.

Her gin journey had been inspired by a tasting session given to her by her son Sam as a gift. By the end of the day, Jacqueline, a part-time music teacher, and Sam had decided to explore the idea of making their own gin, and JacqSon was soon formed.

She ordered her distillery equipment, set it up in her daughter Natasha's old bedroom, brought in her husband Peter as chief taster and started to experiment with flavours.

The original JacqSon Yorkshire Dry Gin recipe went through 24 versions

before she found the flavour she was looking for. It uses ten botanicals and the sweet-tangy rhubarb-liquorice pairing is smooth enough to sip neat, as well as being a great long drink with tonic – or ginger ale. The bottle design is inspired by the rhubarb.

In its footsteps have followed Star Anise & Chilli Gin and Strawberries & Cream Gin; both illustrate Jacqueline's quest for unique flavours.

She found she only needed a small amount of star anise as vacuum distillation intensifies its aniseed flavour, which is then warmed by the chilli. The vacuum distillation also makes its mark in the Strawberries & Cream Gin. Here the fat molecules are removed from the cream, allowing it to be distilled like traditional botanicals. The 42% ABV gin is clear and has hints of vanilla besides its strawberry flavour.

Jacqueline's inventiveness knows no bounds, and she has been commissioned to make gin for other people.

There's King Billy and Beverley gins for Sharron Davis in East Yorkshire, Beerhouses Gin for a pub group in West Yorkshire and Citra Gin – using Citra hops – for Mallinsons brewery in Huddersfield. There is also a spiced rum.

Creating original flavours is the part Jacqueline particularly enjoys. Her daughter may not have a bedroom at the family home, but she did have bespoke lychee and ginger gin favours at her wedding.

JP ADLAM
[JP Adlam No 8]

Gargrave, North Yorkshire
jpadlamgin.co.uk
First gin: September 2018

Creating a distillery is all about getting the foundations right, and Gary Coates and Jason Adlam certainly had plenty of experience from the construction industry to draw on. Gary has worked in the building business for more than two decades, while Jason owns a large Yorkshire-based construction company.

The friends might have hatched the idea in 2017, but after that the focus was on building the right environment to create the perfect gin.

Gary, who already had experience in brewing beer, expanded his knowledge with a course run by the Scotch Whisky Society and industry experts in Edinburgh. It was then a matter of experimenting with flavours, finding suitable property, designing a brand and navigating plenty of red tape.

Their two families formed the LuJo Distilling Company – named after Gary's children Lucy and Joseph – and converted an industrial unit in Gargrave, a large village in the Aire Valley on the edge of the Dales.

The distillery's 300-litre copper still – Lucy May, after Gary's daughter – was built to LuJo's specification in China.

It took seven attempts on a 25-litre still before Gary found the flavour profile for LuJo's signature JP Adlam No 8 gin.

Using juniper, coriander, orange and lemon peels, cubeb peppers, grains of paradise, star anise and Yorkshire lavender, the gin takes on a different taste depending on the type of tonic water it is paired with.

With Indian tonic, the peppery notes emerge, while Mediterranean tonic unleashes the oranges and lemons and elderflower tonic unlocks the lavender.

The traditional London Dry-style gin is distilled, bottled, labelled and wax sealed by hand, and Gary continues to develop further flavours and styles of gin.

Limited editions using No 8 have included blackberry, raspberry and grape gin and an autumnal apple and blackberry gin made with apples from Jason's orchard.

LICKERISH TOOTH DISTILLERY
[Sheep's Eye, Harbinger, Kure, Ginger Ninja]

Lythe, North Yorkshire
www.thelickerishtooth.com
First gin: December 2015

In terms of drama, Lickerish Tooth has it in bucket loads. The name comes from the 1950 Broadway musical *Guys and Dolls*, and the brand takes inspiration from the medieval plague doctors.

The idea of a distillery was the result of two men from Marske enjoying a drink, who fancied making their own.

Ste Donnelly and Peter Thompson's musings on that night led to Ste and his wife Tracey taking up the project.

Lines from Frank Loesser's song *More I Cannot Wish You* when the

grandfather urges the heroine to follow her heart and he hopes her true love will have "the sheep's eye and the lickerish tooth" – and desire her – gave Ste ideas for a name.

They also needed something to make the product stand out and hit on the idea of having a logo of a masked plague doctor.

It seemed a good fit especially as the French word for plague is peste – an amalgamation of Peter and Ste's names – and "masked" sounds like their home town. What's more, the plague doctor's mask would have contained herbs and spices – or botanicals.

Ste, who had worked in health and safety and production, had recently returned from Abu Dhabi and setting up the distillery was an ideal project for him.

His first gin used the other part of the lyric – Sheep's Eye – for its name. It is a traditional London Dry gin, quite sweet and floral on the nose, with the juniper coming through, followed by notes of black pepper, rosemary and thyme from the ten botanicals.

Ginger Ninja was inspired by redhead Ste's childhood nickname. His aim was a new take on London Dry gin with ginger tones alongside strong juniper notes. The versatile Ginger Ninja has become a customer favourite.

The Kure is a lighter, floral gin, with citrus, lavender, cucumber, rocket and cardamom among its botanicals.

In contrast, the Harbinger is a Navy Strength gin with strong flavours from 14 botanicals – including black pepper, lemongrass, fennel seed, ginger root and cardamom – to match its 57% ABV.

Each Lickerish Tooth bottle is a drama in its own right. Wax-sealed with the stamp of the masked plague doctor, they each have a small lucky toad charm at the neck.

This is another nod to the plague doctors who wore a dead toad around their necks to ward off the disease.

In the autumn of 2019, Lickerish Tooth moved into a former farm vehicle repair shop in the village of Lythe near Whitby where, beside the new distillery, a gin school is due to open in 2020.

The Donnellys have taken the opportunity to bring in two new 150-litre stills to join Sarah, the 400-litre Portuguese copper pot still that had been centre stage of their previous set-up at Egton.

LOCKSLEY DISTILLING CO
[Sir Robin of Locksley, VSOT]

Sheffield, South Yorkshire
www.locksleydistilling.com
First gin: July 2014

Stainless steel is a hero product for Sheffield. Invented in the city in the 1870s, it means we have rust-free cutlery to eat with and hygienic vessels to prepare food and drink in. The Portland Works in the city's Highfield area is where the first stainless steel cutlery was manufactured. And it is here, in a 250-litre stainless steel iStill, that Locksley Distilling makes its gin.

A distillery had been a long-held dream for John Cherry who had been fascinated by the craft distilling scene while he was living in New York. With extensive experience in the drinks industry, John and his American wife Cynthia decided to move to England to set up a gin business.

John, who was born and bred in Sheffield, turned to a local hero for the gin's name. Robin of Locksley is often recorded as the figure behind the legendary outlaw Robin Hood. He is said to have been born in Loxley, now a modern suburb of Sheffield.

When it came to the gin, John was looking to create something he could sip neat and, after more than 100 attempts, decided his 61st recipe was the one. Neither a London Dry nor Old Tom-style gin, it is clean, smooth and versatile – it works well on its own or as part of a cocktail.

The botanicals, which include elderflower, dandelion and pink grapefruit, are soaked in a British wheat-based spirit before distillation.

Sir Robin of Locksley Gin was initially made for the Cherrys, but soon they moved into the Portland Works and opened the distillery in 2017. Here, as part of the community of artisans who operate Portland Works as a co-operative, John and his team distil, bottle and label their gins and, since 2019, have welcomed students to their gin school.

The gin's label, designed by Hush Creative in Cornwall, incorporates emblems associated with Robin Hood's skills as an archer. The bespoke embossed bottles are from Allied Glass in Leeds.

John's experimentation has continued: the original has been infused with Real Raspberry & Cardamom for a natural pink gin and he has innovated around the Old Tom style.

The VSOT (Very Special Old Tom) is both Navy Strength and an Old

Tom. Not content with this unusual combination of high strength and sweetness, John has also aged VSOT in wine barrels for limited edition releases. The first edition used a Sauternes barrel, the next a Banyuls which saw the gin take on a rose gold colour from the dessert wine of the Pyrenees.

John has also worked with clients to co-create bespoke gins and, at Cynthia's behest, created Morocello, a Moro blood orange citrus liqueur.

Their aim is to operate the distillery with an ethical, environmental and high-quality ethos, using local, organic, Fair Trade or Fair Wild products where possible.

MASONS DISTILLERY
[Masons Dry Yorkshire Gin]

Leeming Bar, North Yorkshire
www.masonsyorkshiregin.com
First gin: June 2013

The new decade opened a fresh chapter in the story of Masons Dry Yorkshire Gin. The family-run distiller has moved into a purpose-built distillery a couple of miles from its original base in Bedale and increased capacity to achieve ambitious growth plans.

As the pioneers of the Yorkshire gin scene, Karl and Cathy Mason have a reputation for being ahead of the game – not only in coming first to the market with a Yorkshire-made gin in 2014, but in pushing flavour boundaries by making unexpected botanical choices.

It was in April 2019 they had to call on their inner strengths as they watched as their distillery burnt down. The fact that Karl, Cathy and their team were able to keep supplies flowing and then move into a new distillery within a year is testimony to their energy and enthusiasm.

Not only is the distillery home to a brand new copper still but it also has a full bottling plant and the company's offices.

The distillery grew out of the couple's love for gin: Karl, who had run an advertising agency, and Cathy, who worked in a school, enjoyed drinking it as the craft gin movement took root in the UK. Their Facebook postings about what they were tasting on a Friday night started to attract a following and they soon wondered if they could make a stand-out gin themselves.

Working with consultants, they developed their own recipe, had it made for them and they launched Masons Dry Yorkshire Gin on World Gin Day in 2013. When they realised its potential, they set up their own distillery in Cathy's home town of Bedale and it grew from there.

The key botanicals for the Original gin are juniper, cardamom, bay leaf, fennel seed, Szechuan pepper, grapefruit and orange which, with pure Yorkshire spring water, create a bold London Dry-style gin.

Two of Masons' Editions gins feature local produce – lavender from the Yorkshire Wolds and tea from Yorkshire Tea, the sister brand to Bettys tearooms and Taylors of Harrogate. Apple, peppered pear and sloe also feature in the Editions portfolio which sits beside a Yorkshire vodka.

A clever design – incorporating Yorkshire's white rose on the base and

shoulder – makes the Masons bottle stand out from the crowd. Launched in 2017, it was designed by Allied Glass in Leeds.

The distilling is looked after by Luke Smith, who successfully kept production running after the fire by guest-distilling the Mason recipes on other people's stills. Having been able to turn to the gin community in its time of need, it's not surprising to find that collaboration has been a long-standing feature for Masons and it has a roll call of gin partners, who include Theakston's brewery, That Boutique-y Gin Company, Yorkshire Tea, and Ripon Cathedral.

MILL HOUSE DISTILLERY
[Kingtree Gin]

Cottingham, East Yorkshire
www.millhousedistillery.com
First Gin: September 2019

Cottingham is said to be one of the largest villages in England once noted for its springs, fisheries, mills and farmland. The community on the outskirts of Hull has changed over the centuries becoming a centre of snuff manufacture in the late 18th century and since the 1970s the home of Swift caravans. In 2019, it became the home of Mill House Distillery and Kingtree Gin.

Named after a grand Georgian House which once stood in the village, Kingtree Gin is the creation of Mill House founder John Cook. It is the result of many months of recipe development as he worked out a process which would retain the full spectrum of flavours from the botanicals he had chosen to use.

John's bespoke method uses some of the vapour-infused practices of a London Dry gin but also involves maceration in isolation of botanicals to ensure that only those elements he desires are extracted.

John, an engineer to trade, called on his wide experience in manufacturing which began with Allied Foods. He had also been a long-standing gin fan – having started drinking it in his late teens when he was playing rugby union and his teammates were downing pints.

Kingtree Gin features ten botanicals including fennel, coriander and peppercorn, juniper and a rare variety of rosemary grown in John's garden. There are also three types of orange peel and two of lemon which add citrus tones to the warming spicy notes.

The gin is made in Barbara, a 40-litre Portuguese copper alembic pot still named after John's aunt who left him some money as he was planning the distillery. Part of his family home, the distillery is on the site of a mill which was mentioned in the Doomsday Book and later had connections with the trade in snuff, the ground tobacco leaves fashionable in English society from the 17th century.

John quickly followed the launch of his signature Kingtree Gin with the Apple Infused Spiced edition and with his love of his liquorice sweets from his birthplace Pontefract in mind, it's likely the root will feature in one of his future creations.

NORTHERN FOX DISTILLERY
[Northern Fox Yorkshire Dry Gin, Honeyberry Gin]

Beverley, East Yorkshire
www.foxgins.co.uk
First gin: May 2019

As distilling debuts go, Northern Fox made a pretty impressive entrance. Not content with opening a distillery and launching a trio of gins, two of its first year's gins are unique – in Yorkshire and probably further afield.

Opening the distillery was the culmination of a dream for Aimee Toomey and Oliver Beniston and it involved major changes in their lives.

Aimee and Oliver had known each other since their teens in East Yorkshire, pursuing careers – and lives – on different continents before setting up home together. Although living in Lancashire, Aimee, who had been a director of a recruitment company in Dubai and Oliver, a microbiologist in the beverage industry, decided they should make their dream a reality in Yorkshire.

Oliver's industry experience meant he was already familiar with distilling techniques, and when he and Aimee started to experiment and develop gin recipes, they focused on the flavours they liked.

Their original garden distillery in Kirk Ella was the inspiration for their Northern Fox brand as the crafty animals would appear as they worked on a small still. Soon it was home to two 30-litre DES copper pot stills from Serbia – and later a 60-litre sibling. Oliver became a full-time distiller in the autumn of 2019 and they moved to a new site in spring 2020.

Northern Fox's launch trio were Yorkshire Dry Gin, Liquorice

Gin and Traditional Pink Gin. Ironically, it is the pink gin that is the one that stands alone in Yorkshire as it is in the style of the cocktail classic and not sweet like the rose-hued gins many producers in the UK are making. It is their signature Dry gin blended with Angostura Bitters, the natural aromatic flavouring made in the Caribbean from a secret recipe since 1824.

The original Northern Fox Yorkshire Dry Gin is classic in style with only six botanicals selected so that their flavours come through individually in its drinking. Juniper, coriander, cardamom, nutmeg, liquorice root and lemon rind are infused for 48 hours with British grain spirit before they meet one of the stills.

The Liquorice Gin is a simpler recipe with only three botanicals allowing the liquorice to be the star of the show. The pair peel the liquorice root themselves for each batch to ensure that the clear gin has a very mellow flavour which lends itself to sipping neat or with ice. For dramatic effect, it is presented in bottles spray-painted black.

Aimee and Oliver's fourth gin is also something of a show-stopper as it uses the honeyberry. Only recently cultivated in the UK, this fruit – which tastes like a cross between a gooseberry and a blueberry – had been made in Scotland into a gin which is no longer on the market. So Northern Fox's Honeyberry Gin is an English first.

The berries come from an East Yorkshire farmer and, as the brand develops, Aimee and Oliver are keen to use more Yorkshire flavours and themes.

PRIORY FARM
[Priory Gin]

Syningthwaite Priory, Wighill,
North Yorkshire
www.prioryvodka.co.uk
First gin: July 2019

Priory Gin stands out on two counts in the gin world. Firstly, it is one of only a handful of gins that are "field to glass" – gins made at a distillery from ingredients grown on the surrounding land.

Secondly, unlike many distilleries which use a grain spirit as the base for their gin, Priory uses potato spirit for its traditional London Dry-style gin.

It features dandelion and burdock roots as well as bitter orange and grapefruit peels, alongside more traditional botanicals – 16 in total – and water from just 13 miles away.

The gin is the brainchild of third-generation farmer David Rawlings, who grows wheat, potatoes and oil seed rape and raises sheep and cattle on land between Tadcaster and Wetherby.

Like many farmers, the question for David of what to do with the crops that do not meet the grade expected by the supermarkets is a tricky one. The rejected "wonky" potatoes can often go to waste.

Fortuitously, Eric Olszewski joined the Priory Farm team at just the right moment, and his boast that Poles make "better vodka than the Russians" chimed with news of potato vodka's success elsewhere in the UK.

The seeds of the venture were born and David, his sister Shirley Wood, Eric and former corporate banker Neville Clements set about creating Priory Vodka.

Using Eric's experience of making moonshine with his grandfather in Poland, a barn was converted, an Austrian copper column still fired up and Priory Vodka launched in 2017.

The still goes by the name of Isabella, one of the prioresses of Syningthwaite Priory, the 12th-century Cistercian priory which once stood on the land.

Not only does the vodka make use of the farm's potatoes, the peelings feed the livestock and, extending the sustainability of the operation, energy comes from solar panels on Priory Farm.

The gin – and a naturally-coloured pink edition – came later. Again, nothing travels far: the bottles are from Allied Glass in Leeds and are adorned with a simple design based on the Priory brand created by local designer James Foster.

R2 DISTILLERS
[Divine Gin]

Holmfirth, West Yorkshire
www.divinegin.com
First gin: November 2016

Gins can say a lot about their creators. You learn about what inspires them, their tastes and their approach to business. This is true in the case of Divine Gin and its distiller Ray Woolhead and his business partner – and wife – Rachel.

So where did the inspiration come from? It dates back to a chat with friends at an American Independence Day party in 2014. In the following two years the idea grew and – after much discussion – Ray enrolled on a course at the Institute of Brewing & Distilling in London and a distillery – and gin – took shape.

They knew they wanted a gin that was both smooth enough to sip and great with tonic or just ice. Creating this "divine drinking experience" took time, with tastings with friends and neighbours before the signature gin's recipe was finalised.

When they were thinking about their brand, wings were always going to be a key part of it. The inspiration can be traced back to their time in the Royal Air Force, where wings were a constant. They were on the aircraft they worked on and on the uniforms they wore. Their design incorporates gold to represent their intention to be the gold standard of gins.

Their launch name "Angel – Gin Divine" was subsequently changed. With Divine meaning "coming from a god", there is neat link to it being a product from God's Own County. With the name change, they also switched to the distinctive slender bottles, which are decorated directly on the glass by the supplier, Allied Glass in Leeds.

Divine London Dry Gin is aromatic and spicy from coriander seeds, grains of paradise, cubeb, cinnamon and liquorice. It is made with Shepley Spring Water, collected weekly from the village which is a mile or so from the distillery.

Divine Raspberry is infused with pure fruit and has no sweeteners, preservatives or sugars. The 40% ABV gin's fruity fresh flavour and pink colour is all from the fruit.

Ray works his distiller's magic in a converted woollen mill on a modern stainless steel column 500-litre still named Frances. He uses a 50-litre still for small batches and recipe development and bottles and labels all the gin himself.

For Ray, a one-time aircraft welder who has built his own house, been a project manager in the energy efficiency industry and worked in Formula One, this hands-on approach to his gin is no surprise.

Like many distillers, Ray likes to experiment – there is Divine vodka – and happily takes on commissions from brand owners to create bespoke products.

Recent collaborations have seen him working with Cartwright & Butler, the Folklore Society and his friend Rugby League player Eorl Crabtree. The Num8er Gin for the former England and Huddersfield Giants prop dials up the oranges and lemons for a citrus flourish. Collaborations like these are set to continue.

RAISTHORPE MANOR
[Raisthorpe Dry Gin]

Wharram, North Yorkshire
www.raisthorpemanor.com
First gin: October 2016

A raspberry gin liqueur – made at a kitchen table from her grandmother's recipe – was just the start for Julie Medforth. It was 2008 and the tipple was served to the guests at the shoot run on the land her family had been farming since the 1970s.

It was so popular that she started to bottle it and ultimately led her – and her son Oliver – to launch a full-strength distilled gin.

Raisthorpe Dry Gin – made at their nearby Thixendale production site – includes watercress, which a century ago was farmed in the area, to give it a unique peppery finish alongside saffron, angelica, orris root and juniper. The 500-litre stainless-steel still, named Sienna, is under the watchful eye of Jane Inman, the head distiller.

It uses water from beneath their land. In this part of the Yorkshire Wolds, the Gypsey Race flows underground through clarifying chalk before it surfaces and continues east towards the North Sea. Not only is this water very pure but legend links the floods of the Gypsey Race to prophetic powers. The Dry Gin is rested in whisky barrels to give Raisthorpe Oak-Aged a smooth, mellow flavour with a hint of vanilla and spice.

The Shimmer range of 40% ABV gins hark back to childhood flavours such as Bubble Gum, Lemon Drizzle, Pear Drop and Juicy Orange. Launched in response to the tastes of Raisthorpe's customers, the shimmer and colour are added after distillation. There is also a subtly pink Rose Gin at 37.5% ABV.

Alongside the full-strength gins, Raisthorpe makes a selection of fruit liqueurs, flavoured spirits, vodka and jams and jellies. The Dry Gin also appears as the house gin at the Wensleydale Heifer in West Witton.

Not content with this line-up of products, there are stacker bottles, a hamper service and the cute-but-practical Tipsy Drink Cards where a miniature is packaged in a witty gift card for easy posting. And there are retail outlets at McArthurGlen near York and Leeds.

In 2018, a range of Yorkshire tonic waters created from all-natural ingredients was launched to make the perfect partner for Yorkshire's growing selection of spirits.

RARE BIRD DISTILLERY
[Rare Bird Gin]

Malton, North Yorkshire
www.rarebirddistillery.co.uk
First gin: October 2017

Malton certainly lives up to its name as Yorkshire's Food Capital. In the past decade, cafes, shops and producers, together with the farmers' markets and events such as the Food Lovers Festival have seen to it that "Made in Malton" is on everyone's lips.

And it's not just food that is made in the market town in Yorkshire's horse-racing country. Rare Bird Gin is right of the heart of it. Based in Talbot Yard – a popular foodie destination – the distillery and gin school fits right in.

Matt and Elizabeth Stewart had a vision of creating fine flavours like those from the artisan producers they had met in the French wine regions of Bordeaux and the Tuscan hills of Italy.

As gin lovers, they wanted to create a thing of exceptional quality – or as the French would say un oiseau rare – a rare bird.

With a 30-year career as a firefighter behind him, Matt was ready for a new challenge and when they found the former stable block at Talbot Yard, it was the ideal place to build their distillery.

In October 2016, Matt commissioned a 300-litre copper still, and with its gleaming body conjuring up the image of the dome of the cathedral in Florence, it was named after the Tuscan city.

The first bottles of Rare Bird were soon hatched and presented in a striking design by Owen Turner of United by Design, a friend from Matt's rugby-playing days. The refreshing London Dry gin has 11 botanicals, including orange, lemon, hibiscus and rosemary. The fruity-citrus edge is tempered with warmth from cardamom and green pepper.

With the signature gin building up a following, Matt came under pressure to branch out, but he only agreed to make a fruit-flavoured gin on the condition that it contained no added sugars or syrup as he wanted to keep the integrity of his products.

A less complex, four-botanical gin is infused with fresh Yorkshire rhubarb and ginger for no fewer than two weeks and the result is a naturally golden-coloured gin with a punch of rhubarb, finished with warm ginger.

More products are likely to be developed by Matt in the future, but meantime he is busy distilling gin or sharing his secrets of making Rare Bird with students at the gin school.

SHEFFIELD DISTILLERY
[Assay Gin]

Chapeltown, Sheffield,
South Yorkshire
www.facebook.com/Sheffield-Distillery
First gin: September 2018

When you have more than 200 whiskies and 100 gins behind the bar, it's not surprising that a landlord's thoughts turn to the idea of setting up his own distillery.

For Paul Menzies and the team at the Commercial Inn at Chapeltown on the northern edge of Sheffield, whisky making was the dream, but when they tried to turn it into reality, they quickly realised that they didn't have the space.

But they could make gin, and the resulting distillery is in a portable one-time building site office, located beyond the carpark of the pub, which also serves real ales and home-cooked food.

In the distillery sit two copper stills: a Portuguese 300-litre still and a 25-litre still, which is known as Obi-Wan and was made by one of the bar staff who is a coppersmith by trade.

Paul Harrison is the distiller. He explains that he, Paul Menzies and Gary Sheriff, a brewer, wanted a gin that was heavy in juniper and really citrusy, and they wanted to use local ingredients.

The recipe they decided on has 18 botanicals including liquorice inspired by nearby Pontefract's famous confectionery.

With approval from the Cutlers Hall to use the city name for the distillery, they named their first gin Assay Gin after gaining permission from the Sheffield Assay Office to use the Sheffield hallmark.

The gin is made in small batches and a vodka has followed. It is made with rhubarb cut from Paul Harrison's garden and roasted with vanilla. It's a flavour which might find its way into a future gin.

GIN

Sheffie
Distille
Est. 20

ASSAY
Fourth Distillation

Hand crafted in our copper pot stills by the banks
of the Blackburn Brook, Chapeltown

ABV

GIN

ASS
Fourth D

Hand crafted in our copper po
of the Blackburn Brook,

70cl

SHINY COWBIRD SPIRIT COMPANY
[Shiny Cowbird gins]

Shipley,
West Yorkshire
shinycowbird.co.uk
First gin: June 2018

What made the owner of a Shipley bar decide to launch a gin called Shiny Cowbird is quite a tale. There are many puns and flashy words, but behind it lies the desire to use the best products to make the best spirits.

Chris Bee and John Bowman have combined their expertise from beer and cider into a company based at Chris's bar, the Fox in Shipley.

Chris, who previously co-founded the Salamander Brewery, branched out and opened the Fox in 2013. With brewing in the blood, he quickly set up the Beespoke Brewing Co at the Fox. John, meanwhile, is the man behind Grumpy John's Cider.

In 2017, they teamed up to hatch the idea of the Shiny Cowbird Spirit Company. The name refers to the South American bird which lays its eggs in the nests of other birds and in the same way John and Chris have used the existing brewing space to nurture their gin.

They use a Mile Hi 26-gallon stainless-steel still which gives them flexibility and the ability to create liqueurs, absinthe, vodka and an award-winning Black Sambuca (using star anise, liquorice and elderberries) alongside their gins.

The gins include their Signature London Dry which is made with juniper, orris root, cinnamon, angelica, coriander and green cardamom

to create a complex but balanced gin.

The Navy Strength adds orange peel to their signature botanicals, while the Rhubarb Gin is made by compounding the Rhubarb Triangle-grown produce for five weeks in the Navy Strength.

All the spirits are presented in distinctive packaging based on a design by Samantha Yates, a stained-glass artist from Saltaire. Her design captures the glossy iridescence of the shiny cowbird.

SING GIN
[Sing Gin]

Kettlesing, near Harrogate,
North Yorkshire
www.singgin.com
First gin: April 2018

A landscape crafted by its rivers, the Yorkshire Dales are filled with natural beauty. Add what man has created – from the humblest of walls to the grandest of stately homes – and it is bursting with glorious inspiration.

Ian Thompson has used that natural beauty to inspire his family gin business. With a practical curiosity and technical expertise from the fire alarms industry, Ian set out on a quest to make a beautiful gin.

He went on a distilling course and returned home one day with the kit for a distillery – a mini copper pot still and plenty of botanicals – and retired to his cellar to experiment.

His wife, Caron, and twin sons, Richard and James, humoured him … until they realised that he was on to something special.

Intent on creating a premium product which would be a legacy for his family, Ian took advice from gin guru Charles Maxwell at the Thames Distillery, who went on to make the initial batches.

Sing Gin has seven botanicals including juniper, mint and orange peel, and since the spring of 2019 it has been made in the Thompsons' own distillery in the village of Kettlesing on the edge of Nidderdale.

Ian had taken inspiration from the land around him for using flax as the signature botanical. Historical records show the village grew it for the

monks of Fountains Abbey, and the Thompsons are now growing their own flax in the distillery grounds.

To make the gin as beautiful and as smooth as possible, Ian chose to use a grape spirit which he sourced from a vineyard in Cognac. Using grape spirit also links the gin back to the earliest juniper spirits, which would have used it because grain was too precious to distil.

The distillery itself has been a family effort: it replaces a piggery and both the twins were hands-on with the build, with James and Ian now the distillers. They crush the botanicals by hand, tend Bella, the stainless-steel and copper still, and bottle the gin.

Sing's branding is based around Ian's original idea that was inspired by a folly beside the lake at the Studley Royal estate, which is also home to Fountains Abbey. It also incorporates a fearsome gargoyle from Studley Royal to protect the gin's secret recipe.

The rich gold and blue image is screen-printed on the bottles for a luxury look and it's no surprise that Sing Gin is stocked by Fortnum & Mason in London.

With no immediate plans to extend their own brand, the Thompsons have made bespoke gins for select clients but are primarily consolidating on what has been an incredible family journey.

SLOEMOTION
[Hedgerow Gin]

Barton-le-Willows, North Yorkshire
www.hedgerow-gin.com
First gin: May 2017

The Yorkshire landscape is uniquely decorated by its stone walls and its hedgerows. One farmer's decision to stop trimming the hedgerows on his land led to a whole new world.

Joff Curtoys, a passionate conservationist who farmed land in the Howardian hills, found that the hedgerows blossomed when he let nature takes its course.

Among the wild riches were sloes – the dark blue bitter fruit of the blackthorn hedges – which when soaked in gin with sugar create the sloe gin made by generations of farmers.

In 2002, Joff and neighbouring farmers created Sloemotion to make Sloe Gin. Since then there has been Sloe Whisky and a range of hedgerow fruit liqueurs, developed under the direction of Joff and family members including his wife Claire and brother Julian.

The full-strength Hedgerow Gin arrived in 2017. The London Dry-style gin features botanicals they find around the hedges – elderflower, rosehip, nettle leaf, crab apple, sloe stones and wildflower meadow hay. It makes a gin with a mellow, fruity dryness, balanced by several floral notes.

Blackberry & Apple and Rhubarb & Raspberry editions have followed, alongside a botanical vodka.

The gin is made on an iStill at their base at Green Farm in small batches and presented in chunky bottles from Allied Glass in Leeds with intricate designs by Zeppo Creative, also in Leeds. The process is overseen by Sloemotion's distiller, Ian Mansell and his team.

The gin's sloe stones are a good example of Sloemotion's approach to the environment as they are recycled from the sloe gin production.

There are plenty of other examples, including the "rescuing" of a hedgerow from a nearby road junction project and the use of the fruit left after making Sloemotion's range of liqueurs to create chocolates and chutney.

The decision at the beginning of the new century to protect the habitat of wildlife by letting the hedgerows grow means the landscape is now full of flowers and fruit which feed the birds and small mammals … and fuel a sustainable business.

SPEIGHT'S GIN
[SP8 Gin, Shibden Valley Gin]

Northowram, near Halifax,
West Yorkshire
www.sp8gin.com
First gin: July 2019

The Shibden Valley was put on the map in 2019 with the broadcast of a BBC drama *Gentleman Jack*. Based around the life of Anne Lister, the 19th-century resident of Shibden Hall, Anne – one of Britain's first lesbians – inherited the distinctive Tudor-fronted manor house from an aunt and left comprehensive diaries chronicling her life.

It is some of her words that are inscribed on Shibden Valley Gin – a special edition created with the custodians of Shibden Hall, which is now open to the public.

The artisan distillery behind Shibden Valley Gin was founded by Peter Speight. Located in the lush, flower-filled gardens of his home on the north side of the valley, in a shed beneath a horse-chestnut tree, Peter, a global security expert, works with a 100-litre copper pot still from Hillbilly Stills in Kentucky to create his small-batch gins. Named Barbara in memory of Peter's mother, the bespoke still has special botanical baskets engineered by his son-in-law and distilling partner Daniel.

It is a true family business, with Peter's son Simon looking after marketing and wife Angie and daughter Victoria involved in recipe development. The women are also responsible for the delicate botanical illustrations on the labels by graphic designer Helen Lodge.

Peter's signature gin Sp8 features 12 botanicals which capture the atmosphere of the distillery garden on a hot summers' day. They include juniper, hibiscus flowers, elderberry, rose petal, wild rosehip, bilberries and rhubarb.

McFade Photography

The signature gin is a base for Peter's triple-distilled fruit gins which uses real fruit juices (not syrups or sweeteners) in the distilling process. Bilberries from the valley and farm-shop rhubarb feature in these intensely flavoured gins. A Shibden Valley special edition – Huckleberry Gin – combines blueberries and bilberries for another summer-inspired edition.

With his eye for detail and interest in flavours, Peter spends many hours developing the recipes. He is particularly keen to use responsibly sourced natural produce from the surrounding area and a pear gin is set to launch in 2020.

SPIRIT OF MASHAM DISTILLERY
[Spirit of Masham Dry Yorkshire Gin]

Masham,
North Yorkshire
corksandcases.com
First gin: April 2017

Masala chai is one of the most popular drinks in the world. Across India, the spiced tea served in small glasses or clay cups is the drink of choice in homes and anywhere people gather.

It was something Derek and Carol Harle fell in love with on their travels. Back home, they never found anything to match.

The couple who had semi-retired in 2006 from senior roles in the food and drink industry, bought the Corks & Cases wine business in 2011 in Carol's hometown. A couple of years later, on a trip to a relative's vineyard in Australia, they tasted a masala chai that matched up to their Indian experiences.

On their return to Yorkshire, they decided to make their own masala chai and sell it from the shop. The liquid is created from a blend of two high-level plantation whole leaf orange Pekoe Ceylon teas and six spices. Some of the peppercorns, cinnamon, ginger, star anise, cloves and cardamom are toasted to release their oils before blending with the tea. Australian eucalyptus honey is then added.

When distiller Gerard McCluskey was smitten by the chai, he decided it would make a great gin. The Corks & Cases team's blind tasting gave his creation a thumbs-up, and the Harles set about finding a space to distil in. A run-down office block on a business park was secured and transformed into a distillery, and they raced to launch Spirit of Masham Masala Chai Gin at the Tour de Yorkshire in 2017.

The distillery is home to Big Stan, a Portuguese 200-litre copper alembic still, and his 20-litre brother Little Stan. Working with Gerard – who had worked for Tanqueray and Masons – as a consultant, Derek and Carol have learned the art of distilling.

The recipe for Masala Chai Gin, which is now known as Spirit of Masham Dry Yorkshire Gin Original, included hops which are a nod to the town's reputation for brewing beers. The Challenger hop adds a citrus note to gin.

The range of London Dry gins includes Chocolate Malt Barley and Classic Gold which take the brewing theme further.

In the Chocolate Malt Barley Gin, the grain used to make stouts, porters and dark beers is deep roasted and combined with organic cocoa, coconut, rosehip and a hint of Italian dark roast coffee. It is a gin with a subtle, dark bitter chocolate note.

Classic Gold is more spicy, with Goldings hops, golden berries, kaffir lime leaves, lemongrass, peppercorns and the peels of lime, orange and pomelo.

Meanwhile, Spirit of Masham Rhubarb gin is a homage to the Yorkshire plant. The main ingredient comes from the Rhubarb Triangle and the Harles' own garden and is matched up with rose petals and ginger.

Innovation never stops for the Harles: they opened a make-your-own Gin Experience in 2018 and are launching a Design Your Own Gin online service. Customers can choose their own botanicals and create their own recipe, then Spirit of Masham makes the bespoke gin and ships it to them. They also make gins for other clients, including their neighbours at the Black Sheep Brewery.

SPIRIT OF SWALEDALE
[Moorland Gin, Hedgerow Pink Gin]

Muker, Upper Swaledale,
North Yorkshire
spirit-of-swaledale.co.uk
First gin: November 2019

High up in the Dales, two of Yorkshire's newest gin makers need not go far to find botanicals. The heather, bilberry and rowan is all around them. There is even wild juniper by their cowhouse-turned-distillery.

Friends Ian Purves and Richard Hammond had been kicking around the idea of making beer – or maybe gin – for some time. They had experimented with "bathtub" gin but they weren't impressed with their efforts. Then, they decided to take the plunge, order a 20-litre alembic pot still and convert the building near Ian's 17th-century longhouse.

They started with a simple juniper-coriander-lemon recipe and, when they found it tasted like gin, they set about designing a gin that captures the spirit of Swaledale. Richard, a former chef and publican, and Ian, a doctor and entrepreneur, were out on the moors one day and could see the

ideal ingredients around them. With Ian calling on his scientific background and Richard on his culinary experience they came up with a bold gin which captures the drama of their dale with its gorges, waterfalls, heather moorlands, stone walls and isolated houses.

Spirit of Swaledale Moorland Gin has 11 botanicals featuring heather, meadowsweet, bilberry leaf, rowan berries, wild thyme, lemon and orange peel and lots of juniper. It is a citrusy, spicy traditional flavour.

It went down a treat in the area and when the landlord of the Farmers Arms in Muker told Ian and Richard that he expected a pink gin from them next, they

turned to the hedgerows for inspiration. Rosehips, rowan berries and raspberries are enhanced by pink peppercorn, nutmeg and ginger for a pink-coloured juniper-heavy spirit with a rich mouthfeel.

Richard and Ian are contemplating new flavours for their gins, with ginger, rhubarb and fennel in their sights. The gins are hand bottled with labels by York-based designer Nik Cann using Ian's photography.

Ian's ambitions for the brand go beyond gin. Having founded a successful health informatics company and worked as a doctor in the Kalahari Desert, he is keen that Spirit of Swaledale creates economic opportunities for the area. There are already branded hats made with wool from Swaledale sheep, and he hopes other products will follow, giving people opportunities beyond farming and tourism.

TAPLIN & MAGEEAN
[Taplin & Mageean Wensleydale Dry Gin]

Leyburn, North Yorkshire
taplinmageean.co.uk
First gin: December 2018

Grabbing the headlines is one way to start a gin business. Chris Taplin and Barry Mageean made the news because they used a legal loophole for their launch party when they didn't have their full licences in place. By serving alcohol on a moving train they kept things legal and made sure Yorkshire knew their Wensleydale Dry gin had arrived.

Doing things in style is typical of the Taplin & Mageean brand, whose distillery is in a prime location, beside the Wensleydale Railway in the popular Dales village of Leyburn. And its launch event was not for one gin … but four.

Hotelier Chris and distiller Barry had set up the business with the aim of using traditional distilling methods and modern engineering techniques to create the highest quality spirits possible.

Barry had been the head distiller at Masons Yorkshire Gin in Bedale, and with a degree in chemical engineering and experience in industry, his expertise in distilling was key in their plans to create small batch gins that were head and shoulders above the competitors.

Barry's aim is to create recipes that linger and evolve, with flavours which creep up on the palate in a specific sequence. This distinct beginning-middle-end profile that a drinker finds is what sets his gins apart. And Barry's secret is in the way he prepares the botanicals and spirit before distillation.

Taplin & Mageean's signature edition, a classic Dry for the gin connoisseur, is juniper heavy and has plenty of citrus, with both dried

and fresh grapefruit zest. The botanicals also include Yorkshire hops, chamomile and spices.

The orange zest and juniper flavours of Spiced Orange is balanced by fig, cranberry, hazelnut, almond and cinnamon, while in Peach Perfect the botanicals include apricot, vanilla, cocoa bean, basil and pink peppercorn, alongside the peach.

Apples grown in Chris's garden together with coriander, elderflower, chamomile and cinnamon make Taplin & Mageean's Elderflower Orchard a personal statement.

The station distillery has three stills, with more on the cards. Wendy is a 100-litre copper alembic pot still handmade in Portugal and Jenny is a 300-litre replica which joined her in the summer of 2019. Ruby, a 5-litre version, is used for the meticulous trials involved in developing recipes.

Barry's allegiance to copper pot stills is due to the fact that, in spite of their long distillation times and small yields, they are able to extract so much flavour from the botanicals.

Having made a splash with its moving launch, Taplin & Mageean regularly runs gin masterclasses aboard a train travelling through the Dales, ending at the railway distillery.

TRUE NORTH BREW CO
[Sheffield Dry Gin, Marmalade, Barnsley Dry, Leeds Gin]

Sheffield, South Yorkshire
truenorthbrewco.uk
First gin: March 2015

Gin makers are always looking for a unique selling point, something special to make them stand out.

In Sheffield, the citizens will tell you the thing that makes the city special is Henderson's Relish. And for Sheffield Dry Gin it is its USP.

The spicy and fruity dark brown sauce made to a secret recipe since 1885, helps to bind the other flavours in the blend of botanicals inspired by the Peak District.

The story goes that a Sheffield student won a bursary to undertake a project that he was "passionate about" and "completely outside his area of academic study".

Robert Jones's passion was to make gin, so he used money from the Sheffield Hallam University's Heller Bursary to buy distilling equipment to set up his own business doing just that.

Ultimately, he took the idea to Kane Yeardley of True North Brew Co who owned the Stancill Brewery and several Sheffield pubs, including the Old House where Robert had discovered the world of gin as he worked behind its bar.

Having created and launched Sheffield Dry Gin, Robert is forging his career elsewhere and the gins are produced by True North's brewer and distiller Dean Hollingworth on two 60-litre copper pot stills.

The botanicals in the signature Sheffield Dry Gin include fennel, cardamom, gentian root, grapefruit and lemon peel, as well as Sheffield Honey and the Henderson's Relish.

Over the years, there has been a flurry of flavours based on the signature gin but usually with the fennel and honey omitted.

In 2019, Rose & Jasmine, Forest Fruits, Spiced Fig & Victoria Plum were added to the core line up of Moorland Berries, Marmalade and Raspberry & Pomegranate … and there are seasonal gin liqueurs and a vodka from the distillery.

Barnsley Dry Gin blends English apple and rhubarb to showcase the harvest of the orchards and allotments of Sheffield's neighbouring town.

Never one to stand still, True North has added a gin school and, in 2019, it bought Leeds Gin from its founder Sara Birkinshaw.

WEST RIDING DISTILLERY
[Waterton's Reserve Gins,
Barnsley Hospice Gin]

Barnsley, South Yorkshire
watertonsreserve.com
First gin: December 2017

Charles Waterton is something of a hero for distiller Dave Owens. A 19th-century environmentalist from Walton near Wakefield, Waterton travelled around the world, and, in particular, to South America, studying plants and wildlife.

A pioneering conservationist, at home he fought a soap manufacturer which was polluting a river, and on his own estate he established what is reputed to be the world's first nature reserve.

Detailed observations of his expeditions and discoveries are said to have inspired future environmentalists such as Charles Darwin and Sir David Attenborough.

Dave, who ran a craft ale bar in Wakefield, became aware of Waterton when he was involved in a sculpture project as part of an initiative to reinvigorate the town centre.

Waterton immediately chimed with Dave – former drinks industry consultant who had also worked in a rum distillery in the Seychelles – as he had been fascinated by nature since childhood.

On his bar at the time he had a rhubarb and mulberry gin infusion. When he read that Waterton's last entry in his journal mentioned two nightingales "singing melodiously in the park" he immediately named the infusion Nightingale Gin.

It was then an encounter with Sara Birkenshaw, founder of Leeds Gin, which led to Dave doing an "apprenticeship" with her to learn the skills he needed to set up his own distillery and create his own gins.

His first was West Riding Classic Dry Gin. It has a strong focus on the classic 19th-century botanicals and includes South American cocoa nibs beside local flavours to celebrate Waterton's passion for exploration and his Yorkshire roots.

Since September 2018, Dave has been making his gin in small batches in hand-made Portuguese copper alembic pot stills – called Florence (60 litre) and Big Flo (100 litre) – in a unit in a former carpet laboratory next to the Nailmaker Brewery.

The gin was originally marketed as Nightingale Gin until March 2019 when Dave obtained permission from – and the blessing of – Waterton's descendants to use the name. The nightingale remains on the Waterton labels designed by Ian Meade from Barnsley.

The range includes Dandelion & Burdock, Rose & Raspberry gins and a special edition for the 25th anniversary of Barnsley Hospice. Yorkshire Rhubarb Fruit Gin celebrates two very local ingredients. The rhubarb comes from the Oldroyd farms in Rothwell and the mulberry is the fruit of the bush the children dance around in the nursery rhyme *Here We Go Round the Mulberry Bush*. Legend has it that the original bush was in the courtyard of Wakefield jail.

Dave has also produced single-batch allotment editions, a marmalade gin with scratch-and-sniff labels and there's a distillery in Berkshire in the pipeline. Charles Waterton was teetotal so, in 2020, Dave is launching the Squire's Blend – an alcohol-free drink.

WHITBY DISTILLERY
[Whitby Gin, Wild Old Tom, Stoker, Barghest]

Whitby, North Yorkshire
www.whitbydistillery.com
First gin: March 2018

Clinging to the rugged east coast, Whitby is steeped in history and has captured the imagination of generations.

To Bram Stoker, the Victorian author, it was a dark gothic landscape worthy of his most ghastly creation Count Dracula. Over centuries, smugglers, fishermen and sailors have known it as a safe haven, while many of us now see it as a sunny holiday destination of pretty shops and history-filled streets.

For Jessica Slater it was home, and her partner York-raised Luke Pentith had spent happy days there as a child. When they started to dream of making gin, they knew it had to be done in Whitby.

The fact they both had successful careers and were living in Manchester was no barrier and after more than a year of gathering expertise, experimenting with recipes and navigating red tape, they went into production.

At first they worked in a tiny utility room at Luke's parents' home, then an isolated old barn, and in 2020 they hope to have their eco-build distillery and visitor centre in the heart of Whitby open to the public.

They make their gin in small batches on three copper reflux stills, the 200-litre Stanley and its 25-litre siblings, Stockwell and Scripps. The bottles are filled, labelled and packaged by hand.

Jess and Luke's signature Whitby Gin is a homage to their home – from its use of local botanicals to packaging referencing the Abbey, Captain Cook and the coast.

To 12 traditional gin botanicals, they add sugar kelp, heather and honey and steep it overnight before distillation. The sugar kelp is responsibly

foraged at Robin Hood's Bay or, when harvesting would not be sustainable, they go to SeaGrown, a farm which cultivates kelp in the waters off Scarborough.

In the summer, they pick heather

flowers on the North York Moors – working with the National Park and the Strickland Estate. The honey is from bees feeding off that heather. The resulting gin has an initial sweetness balanced with a salinity and the warm notes of heather and juniper.

More ingredients collected by the pair go into their special editions. Blackberries and bay leaf create a rich maroon Bramble & Bay Gin, while gorse and gooseberry, together with a touch of honey, make the Wild Old Tom.

Limited editions celebrate Whitby's association with Dracula which draws Goths to the town. First it was the Stoker Edition – a blackberry and ginger gin – limited to 199 bottles (the number of steps Dracula bounded up as a hound when he arrived in Whitby).

In 2019, the Barghest made a fleeting appearance. Named after the mythical black hound that roams the cobbled streets, Whitby Gin is rested in new barrels of Transylvanian oak for a month and two days (the length of Dracula's voyage to Whitby). It is then gorged in blackberries and ginger. Almost black to the naked eye, once diluted it takes on a blood-red hue which Dracula would surely appreciate.

WHITE HOUSE DISTILLERY
[White House Gin]

Otley, West Yorkshire
whitehousedistillery.co.uk
First gin: October 2019

Otley was once said to have the greatest number of pubs per head in England. The inns were down to the busy markets of the Wharfedale town. Today it still has a large selection of pubs – and there is now a distillery to supply them with gin.

Having started as a gin fan and developed his knowledge, Nick Jocelyn progressed to researching what would be required to set up a distillery and make a good gin. He attended a Brew School distilling course in Derbyshire and worked out how to navigate the red tape that would be involved.

As Nick is a one-time chef, the flavour of the gin was always going to be important to him and his partner Nicola Brown, whose grandfather worked for Gilbey's Gin. They experimented on a mini still and worked with craft distilling consultant Jamie Baxter to refine their recipe.

The result is the citrusy, London Dry-style White House Gin. It has 13 botanicals with liquorice, cardamom, nutmeg and chamomile among them, alongside pink grapefruit and lemon peel.

Getting this gin into the bars of Otley – and further afield – was not without its challenges. As Nick was determined to make his gin in the town, he needed a suitable space, and it took him two years to find the store room in a former textile mill which is now the distillery. It is home to Guido, a 250-litre G-Still with vapour column and it is where Nick hand bottles his gin.

The still's name is a nod to Guy Fawkes, who was descended from the Fawkes family of nearby Farnley Hall, and the distillery is named after the White House on Otley Chevin, which Nick can see from his home.

Nick's focus on the Otley area means he has tried to source as much as he can locally. Printed in Pudsey, the dramatic labels are by graphic

designer Giles Walker, who lives on the Chevin and embraced the project from the start. They incorporate both the White House and an early map with it marked on it. The bottles are from Allied Glass in Leeds.

Nick has invested in a laser engraving machine which means he can personalise his bottles. And almost immediately after launch he was being commissioned to produce special editions of White House Gin.

In the future, Nick can see himself looking at summer fruits for a gin and perhaps diversifying into other spirits.

WHITTAKER'S DISTILLERY
[Whittaker's Gin, Pink Particular,
Winter Solstice, Summer Solstice]

*Dacre Banks, near Harrogate,
North Yorkshire*
www.whittakersgin.com
First gin: July 2015

Yorkshire Day 2019 marked a major milestone for Toby Whittaker on his distilling journey. It was the day of the official opening of his new distillery, only a couple of steps away from his original set-up in a former piggery.

It is a purpose-built home for Toby's new American stills, a café and shop right in the heart of Nidderdale.

The journey began when he and his wife Jane decided to create a small-batch gin which reflected the Yorkshire countryside. Initially, the couple, who had experience in property management, had been looking to start a microbrewery.

When they visited the International Centre for Brewing and Distilling at Heriot-Watt University in Edinburgh they changed direction. For Toby, who had studied chemistry at university, it was the perfect project.

They installed a 100-litre American still in a pig shed at Harewell, their

home, commissioned designs based on the animal in its name – a hare – and went into production. Later they added stills made by Tadweld in Tadcaster.

The signature botanicals of the Original Gin are inspired by the bounty of the Yorkshire landscape. Bilberries are abundant at nearby Brimham Rocks, while hawthorn berries adorn the hedgerows. Bog myrtle, which grows on the moors, adds both bitter and balsamic notes to the traditional gin botanicals of juniper, coriander, angelica root and lemon, and thyme is picked fresh from their garden.

The berries are macerated for 24 hours before a London Dry distillation. The spirit is diluted using water from the Harewell water source and left to settle before being

hand bottled, batch numbered and labelled. The hare design on the label is based on a wood engraving by the 18th-century naturalist Thomas Bewick.

Further editions of Whittaker's Gin have celebrated the seasons – Winter Solstice and Summer Solstice – or more local ingredients such as in the Sloe with Honey Gin, which used honey from a beekeeper in Summerbridge.

For the Navy Strength, Toby identifies the ideal time to retain some of the signature gin as it runs off the still. The spirit alters slightly through the distillation run, and this finely judged portion is then diluted to the traditional 57% ABV of Navy Strength.

There are also bespoke gins made for other people including Fortnum's English Cassis Gin, Double Sloe Gin for That Boutique-y Gin Company and Greystone Gin for the Harewood Food & Drink Project.

The new distillery, designed and built by local craftsmen, is home to three American stills including a 500-litre copper gin still named, like all of its predecessors, Jezebel after Toby and Jane's daughters, Jessica and Isabella.

This set-up will allow Toby to make his own neutral grain spirit from grain grown in the neighbourhood, as well as to make whisky. With a range of sustainable features, it paves the way to Whittaker's being a grain-to-glass craft distillery.

YORK GIN COMPANY
[York Gin, Outlaw, Roman Fruit]

Acaster Malbis, York
www.yorkgin.com
First gin: March 2018

As the modern gin craze has grown, there has been a succession of gins honouring their hometowns. York was not one of them – until five of its residents set about putting that right.

They had plenty of material to inspire them, as York Gin's cat and castle logo testify.

The original York Gin is a classic London Dry, using traditional botanicals including juniper, coriander, orris root, cardamom, grains of paradise, black pepper, cinnamon, lemon peel and angelica. These are ingredients that would have been available in York during the 18th-century Gin Craze.

With the company motto "History in the tasting", it's not surprising that York Gin has plundered the history books for inspiration.

Roman Fruit uses plants associated with the Romans – some of the city's most influential former residents. A fruit tea that includes strawberry, raspberry, apple and hibiscus is infused with the original gin after distillation. There is no sugar added and it remains at 42.5% ABV.

The Navy Strength Outlaw pays homage to the city's notorious characters such as Guy Fawkes, Dick Turpin and Mary Bateman, the Yorkshire Witch.

York's popular cat statues meant a feline figure was already a feature on the gin label and with the cat the sign of the 18th-century sellers of sweetened gin, an Old Tom edition of York Gin was inevitable.

Its sweetness comes from a herb-infused sugar syrup made in the kitchen of the Michelin-starred Star Inn at Harome. The syrup's ingredients include white alba rose – the one on the Yorkshire flag – bronze fennel, star anise, angelica and pink peppercorns.

There have been other York-inspired gins – for the Theatre Royal and to celebrate the city's chocolate industry – and more are likely in the future.

When you consider York's rich history it was obvious to the founders of

80 · YORKSHIRE'S GINS

the York Gin Company that the city needed its own gin. Four friends had been laying the foundations for the project, when marketer and gin lover Emma Godivala, who was also investigating the idea, tried to register the name. She realised she already knew the four – Paul Crossman, Pete McNichol, Harry Cooke and Jon Farrow – and so they teamed up.

In spite of a pause after Jon's sudden death, the team brought their various expertise together to create a gin that celebrated York.

Head distiller Harry took an idea on a scrap of paper to make a carefully designed classic distillery built around a bespoke 300-litre copper still, Ebor – an abbreviation of the Latin name for York.

Although deeply rooted in the past, the distillery looks to the future with a sustainable approach using renewable energy and recycling waste, and the gins contain no animal products.

In 2019, with the distillery in a former chicken shed on the outskirts of the city, York Gin opened a shop in the city centre at Sir Thomas Herbert's House on Pavement.

YORKSHIRE DALES DISTILLERY
[Purple Ram, Desert Ram, Wild Ram, YD]

Colburn,
North Yorkshire
www.yorkshiredalesdistillery.com
First gin: February 2017

Military precision and discipline go a long way in distilling. Attention to detail and routine in the distillery can make all the difference to the spirit which comes off the still. Tony Brotherton and his wife Sarah have called on his military background in many ways as they set up a craft distillery to produce a range of spirits.

In addition, Tony, who served in the Royal Artillery for 18 years, has been able to support the armed services that gave him a career. The distillery has signed the Armed Forces Covenant, joined the Defence Employer Recognition Scheme and prioritised the employment of forces veterans, as well as the long-term unemployed, young people and ex-offenders. In 2019, there were five members of staff who fitted those criteria.

Based on the doorstep of Catterick, the UK's largest military garrison, the distillery is in a former wine warehouse which fits its new purpose perfectly. The 30-litre and 500-litre stills have no-nonsense names – Little Still and Big Still – and can be reconfigured to make a range of spirits.

It may seem an unusual second career for Tony, but when you learn that his father worked with distilleries creating and developing stills and engineering equipment and hear that he was once caught brewing beer at school, you realise he seemed destined to this life.

Not content with his practical experience, Tony has been studying for his masters degree at the International Centre for Brewing and Distilling at Heriot-Watt University in Edinburgh.

His first gin was a classic London Dry. Purple Ram has floral and citrus notes from juniper, pink grapefruit peel, honey from hives less than a mile from the distillery and another seven botanicals. It is vapour infused, quadruple distilled and diluted with water from a natural aquifer in Swaledale.

Having served in North Africa and the Middle East, Tony's "army strength" edition is Desert Ram Gin. Made with cardamom, rose petals and bitter orange, with succulent dates to intensify its creaminess, the 50% ABV edition

evokes the flavours of those places. Wild Ram adds berries – gooseberry, redcurrant and blackcurrant – from Thirsk to Yorkshire heather in an exceptionally dry, juniper-led gin.

They are presented in bottles bearing a line drawing of a ram which symbolises Yorkshire and stands for integrity, independence and resilience – characteristics the distillery aspires to.

At the end of 2018, the YD range of full-strength contemporary gins was launched with a look that has a completely different vibe. For the gins, the fruit is distilled and only the minimum amount of sugar is added. Strawberry & Thai Basil, Honeyed Rhubarb, Bramble Berry gins stand alongside a Spiced Golden Rum.

In the distillery's repertoire there are also vodkas and rums, as well as bespoke gins made for clients which range from battalions to shops.

To cope with the success that the Yorkshire Dales Distillery has seen, an expansion of the operation and the creation of a visitor centre are on the cards.

THE KITH & KIN

Kith (one's friends or acquaintances) and Kin (one's relatives)

The Kith & Kin are the gins and makers who didn't make it to the Distilling Clan. They come from a variety of backgrounds across Yorkshire – and beyond.

There are also gins created in Yorkshire but made by someone else in an established distillery. The creators of these gins might be making them for shops, hotels, visitor attractions or events. For others, they are commercial brands. Some of the gins use botanicals hand picked from their home area or they might be inspired by the creator's heritage. These gins are made both in Yorkshire and elsewhere. They have all been included so that you can make up your own mind.

Bathtub gin doesn't require a still to make it, so these makers are included here. They cold-compound botanicals or fruit usually over a number of months to create gins bottled at a minimum of 37.5% ABV (alcohol by volume).

There are sure to be omissions. Not only are new gins launched with amazing regularity, but some successfully hide their light under the proverbial bushel.

THE ARTFUL POUR

Yeadon, West Yorkshire
theartfulpour.com
Launched: July 2018

Style is everything for the creators of the Artful Pour range of gins. Inspiration comes from the entertainment and enjoyment associated with Yorkshire's Victorian theatres.

The Yorkshire Dry is as dry as the Yorkshire wit, with a classic juniper-rich flavour and undertones of lavender, while the nippy-sweetness of English Rhubarb brings sharp drama to the stage.

Devised by media man Andrew Myers and Carl Hopkins who has worked in the gin business, the Artful Pour started out as a quintet of gins.

The debut line-up was completed by Pink Grapefruit, Cucumber & Mint and Violet gins. Each one makes a dramatic entrance with an unforgettable flavour: the sharp citrus of the grapefruit, the cool combo of the cucumber and mint or the Violet's evocation of childhood Parma violet sweeties.

The Artful Pour's five became six with the arrival in 2019 of Passion Fruit which is full of tropical notes from a particularly high proportion of its key fruit.

All the gins have 100 per cent natural ingredients, no added sugar and are bottled at 40% ABV. They are handmade in small batches for the Leeds duo by Dominic M'Benga of Hooting Owl Distillery at Barmby Moor in East Yorkshire.

BAR WALLS GIN

York
www.barwallsgin.co.uk
Launched: December 2018

In York, a bar does not necessarily mean what a gin drinker might think. Although the city is legendary for having a pub for every day of the year, it also has some more unusual bars. These bars are the gateways to the city through its medieval walls. Replacing earlier defences, the distinctive 13th-century limestone walls have protected the citizens – from the Scots, in the English Civil War and latterly from ravages of modern urbanisation.

Walmgate Bar wears its defensive role proudly with its barbican in place and what are thought to be the scars of military attacks. In peaceful times, the bars would have been meeting places and Micklegate was a focus for grand events and revelry.

Gin enthusiasts Dan and Claire Sykes have celebrated York's bars with a pair of gins. They had amassed a substantial collection of gins, and, working in the food industry, they became intrigued by the idea of creating their own gin using botanicals that they had grown themselves. Living close to York, they also looked at botanicals introduced by the Romans who left such a legacy in the city.

Made by the Yorkshire Dales Distillery, the two Bar Walls gins use the same botanicals – juniper, orange peel, coriander, sweet cicely, lemon thyme and ginger mint – but in different quantities. This creates two quite distinctive gins.

The Micklegate edition is a smooth sipping gin which drinks well neat. Sweet cicely adds slight aniseed notes with the ginger mint giving a little zing to what is predominantly a citrus gin. With more lemon thyme and orange peel, the Walmgate edition is more suited to a Mediterranean tonic for a longer drink. The sweet cicely, ginger mint and lemon thyme are grown by Dan and Claire just eight miles from the city walls.

Watch out in future for gins in honour of Monkgate and Bootham bars.

BEVERLEY GIN

Beverley, East Yorkshire
www.kingbillygin.net
Launched: December 2018

Beverley is one of Yorkshire's most attractive market towns. Many people know it for the magnificent minster or the exhilarating flat racing, but it also notable for its fine Georgian architecture and its shopping experience.

The gothic Beverley Minster is regarded as one of the most beautiful churches in England. The 13th-century ecclesiastical masterpiece keeps watch over a town enlivened by thriving traditional markets, upmarket shops and a variety of eating and drinking venues. The horseracing is a spectacle that attracts thousands of people each summer to the course on Beverley Westwood.

Celebrating the charms of the town is Beverley Gin. It has been created by East Yorkshire businesswoman Sharron Davis, the owner of King Billy Gin.

Beverley Gin is light floral gin which combines the delicate hint of rose petals with the berry-rich warmth of hibiscus. Lemon peel adds overtones of citrus, while chamomile's gentle sweetness softens the classic gin which is made for Sharron by Jacqueline Dumigan of JacqSon in Huddersfield.

The bottle features an illustration by Sharron that cleverly captures the charms of the town in words and pictures. Sharron, who has loved art and design since childhood but has no formal training, creates illustrations with words relating to the subject of each piece.

BLACK SHEEP YORKSHIRE DRY GIN

Masham, North Yorkshire
www.blacksheepbrewery.com
Launched: October 2019

The Theakston name is one of the best known in Yorkshire's brewing history. When one member of the family decided to break out on his own, he used the name Black Sheep.

Since 1992, when Paul Theakston took the bold step of setting up his own brewery, the fifth-generation brewer has seen it flourish into one of the country's most respected independent beer-makers.

The cornerstone of the brewery's approach has been progression, quality and authenticity, and when Paul's sons Rob and Jo, who now run the operation, were looking to expand into spirits, they continued this philosophy, keeping things local and artisan.

They have partnered with their neighbour, the Spirit of Masham Distillery, and Black Sheep Yorkshire Dry Gin is the result.

Their modern take on a classic London Dry-style gin is strong on citrus with lemon, orange, apricot, elderberry and pomelo peel among the 14 botanicals, alongside pink peppercorns and juniper.

What makes it the perfect fit for the brewers at Black Sheep is its finish of malt barley and lemondrop hops.

The gin is made in small batches in a copper alembic still and although the peppercorn gives it a bite, it is smooth enough for sipping neat.

The label is designed around a specially commissioned woodcut representation of the brewery's iconic sheep by Andrew Davidson.

Expect the Theakstons to expand their range of Black Sheep spirits in the future.

CAMPBELL'S OF LEYBURN

Leyburn, North Yorkshire
www.campbellsofleyburn.co.uk
Launched: July 2018

An integral part of Leyburn in Wensleydale is R Campbell & Sons. Founded in 1868, there have been five generations of the Campbells involved in keeping the Dales community fed and watered at this popular one-stop shop.

Although a long-standing feature of the town, Campbell's has not been afraid to move with the times. As it approached its centenary, the traditional store was transformed into a self-service shop – the first in the Dales.

Today, alongside the convenient items of everyday life, it puts the emphasis on artisan products. It boasts not only a cheese counter to die for and a speciality butcher, but it also has a treasure trove of wines and spirits.

True to its reputation for helping artisans and small manufacturers get their products into the marketplace, it has an impressive line-up of craft gins.

In 2018, as the shop celebrated its 150th year in business, owner Kath Campbell, store manager Richard Walker and distiller Tony Brotherton of Yorkshire Dales Distillery at Catterick

decided to create a bespoke gin. They chose a blend of fresh and citrus flavours developed from local herbs partnered with Yorkshire honey and heather. It uses natural mineral water from Swaledale.

The traditional honey is produced not ten miles away in Hipswell by Kath's partner Peter Russell, and Kath is often on hand to help look after the bees.

Such a success was the celebratory spirit that it continues as the store's signature gin.

CARTWRIGHT & BUTLER DARJEELING INFUSED PARLOUR GIN

Gilberdyke, East Yorkshire
www.cartwrightandbutler.co.uk
Launched: October 2019

Produce in some of the most prestigious grocery stores in London comes from a family business in Yorkshire. Selecting the perfect delicacies for afternoon tea in Harrods or Selfridges, you will probably consider Cartwright & Butler products.

The distinctive clip-top containers are filled with all sorts of goodies – from tea leaves to biscuits, preserves and chutneys. Based near Beverley, Cartwright & Butler also supplies many other shops across the world and has a range of luxury hampers as well.

The Arnett family, which now owns the company, has a strong heritage of baking, with Gordon Arnett's Cake Shop opening in Beverley in 1946. Today, Cartwright & Butler aims to ensure that the British teatime table is groaning with the finest of treats.

To enhance that luxury experience, the family wanted to create a gin that would be the perfect accompaniment to the traditional afternoon tea.

With the cup of tea being at the centre of this ritual, the obvious ingredient for a gin was one of its teas. Having toured the plantations of the world to find the teas which go into its exclusive blends, the Cartwright & Butler team knew that it had some great botanicals to work with.

Collaborating with Ray Woolhead of Holmfirth-based craft distillery R2 Distillers, they chose Darjeeling which is one of the teas in Cartwright & Butler's Delicate Afternoon Blend.

The champagne of teas, Darjeeling, has a delicate taste – a light, musky spiciness – which doesn't overtake the flavour of the gin. The company's acacia honey is the gin's other hero ingredient.

In total, the gin has 11 botanicals

including juniper, coriander, angelica, cassia, orris root, lemon peel and spices and it uses spring water sourced from Shepley near the distillery.

The cork-sealed bottle arrives in one of Cartwright & Butler's signature tins. Inside is the lightly-zested refreshing Darjeeling Infused Parlour Gin.

DOWNTON ABBEY GIN

Ripley, North Yorkshire
www.harrogatetipple.com
Launched: August 2019

Television has certainly helped spread the fame of Yorkshire. Whether it is *Emmerdale*, *All Creatures Great and Small*, *Last of the Summer Wine*, or more recently *Downton Abbey*.

Downton Abbey, the tale of the aristocratic Crawley family and their servants, is set in a fictional area somewhere north of Harrogate in the rich North Yorkshire countryside.

As the movie of the hugely popular TV series hit the cinemas in September 2019, the licensed Downton Abbey Premium Gin debuted on the shelves, with a whisky co-star.

The gin is made by master distiller Tom Nichol at Harrogate Tipple, the distillery at Ripley Castle, a setting which could almost be a shoo-in for Downton.

Using botanicals from the castle's gardens and hothouse which evoke the era of Downton, the gin has a citrus burst alongside notes of rose. The key botanicals include fresh limes and ginger root, as well as English rose water and Harrogate Spring Water.

Watch out for the appearance of an English Pink Rhubarb edition of Downton Abbey Gin in 2020.

COCKTAIL BAR   EVIL EYE   GIN SHOP

EVIL EYE

Online
eyegin.co.uk

Buy Online
www.evileyegin.co.u

EVIL GINS

Evil Eye Lounge, York
www.evileyegin.co.uk
Launched: September 2017

It's the gin shop everyone is talking about. Evil Eye in the heart of York is the place to go for its choice of gins. In fact, Guinness World Records recognises it for having the "most varieties of gin commercially available".

When gin lover Shelley Green bought the shop and cocktail bar in 2011, it already stocked a wide range of spirits, but in January 2017 she decided to turn her passion into a business strategy and quickly expanded the number of gins on the shelves.

Customers flocked to the small shop in Stonegate, and by 2018 its fame was boosted when the world record recognised its 1,028 gins. At the last count the number of gins totalled 1,300.

As the bottles of gin stacked up, Shelley created her own range of Evil Gins. She then commissioned Dominic M'Benga of Hooting Owl Distillery at Barmby Moor to make them.

First was SG – using liquorice, aniseed and salted sweet orange – and SL – a savoury Mediterranean-influenced gin. SG was inspired by Shelley's memories of her mother returning from Copenhagen laden with Danish salted liquorice and is sweet and herbaceous.

SL was created by Stefano Lombardo, the Evil's Sicilian bartender in chief. He was inspired by the flavours of his home and the botanicals include basil, oregano, rosemary, orange peel and sun-dried tomato.

In 2019, the Mother and Father of All Evil gins followed. Created by Shelley's mother, the 42% ABV Mother of All Evil is a London Dry-style juniper-led gin with a bit of a kick from citrus and saline undertones from fresh bladderwrack.

It is Shelley's stepfather who is responsible for the complex Father of All Evil. The botanicals include kaffir lime, lime peel and cardamom along with secret spices for an "explosion of zest".

FOLKLORE SOCIETY

Leeds, West Yorkshire
folkloresocietygin.com
Launched: October 2017

The Folklore Society has almost created its own legend – a gin that is as local as can be. Initially conceived by three characters of the Leeds gin community – Nolan Kane of Allied Glass, Sara Birkinshaw, the founder of Leeds Gin and designer Barry Darnell – it is a London Dry gin which showcases the area's resources and talent.

The signature gin created by Sara for the Folklore Society is a classic London Dry style, featuring hand-picked plums, as well as figs and English coriander seeds.

It is presented in elegant bottles from Allied Glass, the bottle manufacturer where Nolan is business development manager.

The label's artwork is based around the legend of the beautiful Lady Sybil of Todmorden Moor. It is a tale of witchcraft, nature, greed and treachery which is said to linger on the moor today.

The artwork was created in the studios of Barry's agency Analogue Creative, the birthplace of design for a roll call of international brands.

The illustration's folk-art style is enhanced on the bottle thanks to Allied's ability to print six colours directly on to glass. A highly specialised decorating machine using thermoplastic inks, which dry instantly, can apply layers on top of each other without smudging.

In 2019, with Sara having retired from Leeds Gin, Ray Woolhead the maker of Divine Gin in Holmfirth, became the distiller. He has reworked the original recipe and has already introduced a Rhubarb and Apple gin, ensuring this modern legend lives on.

GRANNY GARBUTT'S GIN

Teignmouth, Devon
www.grannygarbuttsgin.co.uk
Launched: August 2017

A Yorkshire gin-loving granny has been the inspiration for the founders of Exeter Gin in Devon.

Karen Skerratt's grandmother was born in Osmotherley in North Yorkshire in 1901 and brought up above the family butcher's shop in Yarm.

She married Alfred Garbutt and raised a family who have happy memories of time spent in grandad's allotment and their "naughty" granny socialising with a G&T.

Karen, her husband Michael and daughter Lyndsey had run a popular pop-up bar – Granny Garbutt's Gin Palace – around Bath and Exeter before they founded Exeter Gin. They launched both Exeter and Granny Garbutt's gins at the same time.

Granny Garbutt's is distilled by Michael using a one-shot method in a traditional 450-litre copper alembic still, named Isabelle after the Skerratts' granddaughter, or one of two 100-litre stills. The bottles are hand filled and labelled.

Its 14 botanicals reflect Granny's moorland roots, with foraged heather and gorse flower alongside marigold flowers and hibiscus which add delicate floral tones and wildflower organic honey for sweet notes.

Grandad's Revenge is Granny's Navy Strength edition, while Allotment Rhubarb Gin takes inspiration from the family's memories of eating the rhubarb which flourished in Grandad's allotment in Yarm.

Exeter Gin celebrates the city's Roman heritage with botanicals such as tarragon, basil, cardamom and marigold which might have been used at the time. There is also a Navy Strength bottling called Ivaar the Boneless.

GREYSTONE GIN

Harewood Food & Drink Project, Leeds
www.harewoodfoodanddrink.com
Launched: March 2017

The Harewood Estate is 4,500 acres of fields, meadows, moors and wetlands to the south of Harrogate. At its heart is the imposing Harewood House, home to the Lascelles family. Built between 1759 and 1771 to the plans of John Carr, its interiors were designed by Robert Adam, with furniture by Thomas Chippendale and portraits by the greatest artists of their times.

The fertile lands of the estate, which stretches north from the edge of Leeds to the River Wharfe, have nourished a rich heritage of food production, with its fruit, vegetables and meat in great demand.

The Harewood Food & Drink Project was founded in 2016 to celebrate and promote that heritage. Its director Eddy Lascelles collaborates with the area's best artisan producers to create bespoke products and experiences (such as pop-up supper clubs) using produce either grown, reared or foraged on the estate.

The project's aim is to blend the estate's traditional Yorkshire roots with a vibrant modern approach that is in tune with today's desire for interesting flavours and local provenance.

One of its first products was Greystone Gin. It is a collaboration with Toby and Jane Whittaker of the Whittaker's Distillery in Dacre, west of Harrogate.

Eddy and Toby looked to the history of the Capability Brown-designed grounds and what grows in them today for inspiration as they developed the recipe.

Greystone Gin uses elderberries foraged from the estate with fruit hand picked from a 100-year-old mulberry bush on the shore of the lake, a focal point of the grounds.

Harewood has glorious heated glasshouses, which were famous for growing pineapples in the times when they were a prized exotic rarity. There were 22 variations of the gin before they found the perfect combination that included the pineapple.

The gin is London Dry style, so all the flavours are created in the small-batch distillation on the Whittaker's copper stills. The mulberry gives a sweetness on the nose, while the elderberry adds sharpness before the hint of pineapple appears at the end. As Eddy says, it is a gin-drinker's gin.

The gin is named after a large rock in Grey Stone Pasture. The rock has a series of concentric circles pecked out on it, probably with a deer antler in prehistoric times, which are incorporated into the label design.

Greystone Gin was launched alongside a beer from the Quirky Ales microbrewery in Garforth which uses hops grown on the estate. Other products from the Harewood Food & Drink Project include venison pies and honey from hives on the estate. In each case the products are simple and sustainable – and provenance is key.

KING BILLY GIN

Hull, East Yorkshire
www.kingbillygin.net
Launched: June 2018

This is a drink which celebrates one of the key figures in gin's history. When William of Orange came to the English throne in 1689, the country was at war with France. As part of the conflict, French goods were banned, meaning supplies of the favourite drink of the time – brandy – dwindled.

In its place the Dutch spirit jenever grew in popularity. It became fashionable not only as a drink, but as a mark of allegiance to the new king. Two acts of Parliament in the early 1690s fuelled the making – and drinking – of juniper spirit in England, so much so that by 1720 the Gin Craze had taken its hold, and gin was firmly established in British life.

When businesswoman Sharron Davis started creating illustrations of Hull's landmarks, she was intrigued by the statue of King William "our Great Deliverer" in Market Place. Astride his golden horse, Sorrel, he is known to Hull's residents as King Billy.

As a gin drinker and learning of the king's role in the growth of gin, Sharron was surprised to find there was no gin celebrating him. She took to social media and found support for her idea of creating a gin in King Billy's honour.

Orange was the obvious ingredient to include and its peel adds a zesty, citrus freshness to the botanicals which include juniper, grains of paradise, vanilla and lavender.

The gin, which is made by Jacqueline Dumigan of JacqSon in Huddersfield, is presented in a bottle with Sharron's illustration of Hull's landmark statue. Hull born and bred, Sharron has loved design since childhood and has started creating illustrations of Hull landmarks with words relating to the subject. It was during her research into King Billy that she spotted the gap in the gin market.

LEEDS GIN

Leeds, West Yorkshire
www.leedsgin.com
Launched: March 2016

Leeds Gin is now in a new phase of its life. Having been founded by Sara Birkinshaw, the company was sold to the True North Brew Co of Sheffield in the summer of 2019.

The new owner is keeping production in Leeds to stay true to its roots, with True North's distiller travelling to the city to use Sara's original 35-litre copper alembic still.

The Original Dry gin uses traditional botanicals including juniper berries, coriander seeds, cassia bark, orange peel as well as ginger, agave and Yorkshire foraged rhubarb.

There is a fruit theme in two of Leeds's other gins, with Apple & Blackberry and Strawberry & Raspberry both packed with berries.

Leeds Gin's reputation for experimentation continues with limited editions pushing boundaries. In Parma Violet, the Original Dry gin is infused with sugared violets, for a real evocation of the past.

True North, which makes the range of Sheffield Dry Gins, has reinforced Leeds Gin's identity as a no-nonsense, straight-talking gin and has redesigned its branding.

Inspired by the Leeds coat of arms which features an owl, a symbol of wisdom and power, the imagery of the bird has been broken down into geometric shapes with bold, contrasting colours by True North's senior designer Anna Pethen.

THE MAN BEHIND
THE CURTAIN GIN

Leeds, West Yorkshire
themanbehindthecurtain.co.uk
Launched: February 2019

When chefs work with distillers, you expect to taste something special. In the case of Michael O'Hare, chef-patron of The Man Behind The Curtain, the idiosyncratic basement restaurant in Vicar Lane, if he was going to put his name to a gin it was always going to be one that pushed boundaries. And when the Michelin-starred chef teamed up with Slingsby Gin the flavour boundary was caviar.

Known for his unusual flavour combinations and eccentric culinary style, Michael partnered with Mike Carthy and Marcus Black of Harrogate-based Slingsby and set about capturing the distinctive style of his cuisine with flavours designed to complement a savoury palate.

The result is that caviar and plankton are distilled and added to Slingsby London Dry Gin to create The Man Behind The Curtain Gin.

The caviar comes from the Exmoor Caviar farm in Devon, which rears sturgeon in cool water naturally filtered through slate, shale and sandstone and its caviar is enhanced by Cornish sea salt.

Slingsby London Dry Gin is made at Langley Distillery in the Midlands with botanicals sourced from the kitchen garden at Rudding Park in Harrogate or further afield in Yorkshire. They include primrose, sweet cicely, nettle, rhubarb, milk thistle and rosehip and the gin uses Harrogate spa water.

MIDSUMMER NIGHTS GIN

*Sutton-on-the-Forest,
North Yorkshire*
www.theyorkshireexplorer.co.uk
Launched: December 2018

Callum Houston runs bars for events and parties all across Yorkshire and beyond. Whether it's weddings, corporate functions or his trademark Land Rover cocktail bar, Callum and his team of Yorkshire Bartenders have become a regular sight at special occasions.

Organising the drinks for so many events, Callum spotted the need for a premium gin that would showcase Yorkshire ingredients. Using his wide experience behind the bar, he launched the Yorkshire Explorer and worked with a distiller to create a recipe which Yorkshire could be proud of.

The company's first gin – Midsummer Nights – uses botanicals grown not far from home. There is lavender from a specialist farm near Castle Howard, roses from allotments close to York and elderflower harvested near Birdsall House.

Together with hibiscus, orange, lime and more traditional botanicals it makes for a floral gin with lingering citrus undertones.

The intensity of the flavour is due to high ratios of botanicals and taking only the purest of the spirit as it comes off the still.

It is presented in a colourful label from United by Design, a York-based agency which is no stranger to the drinks industry.

The autumn of 2019 saw the launch of Wild Winter Berry – a dry gin with notes of sloe, damson plums and blueberry finished with Douglas fir and lemon peel – and you can expect further seasonal releases in the future.

The gins are made for Callum at the Yorkshire Dales Distillery at Colburn, near Catterick.

MILITARY SPIRIT GIN

Catterick, North Yorkshire
militaryspirit.co.uk
Launched: September 2018

Through the centuries, the military has left its mark in Yorkshire. From the Vikings and Saxons, through the War of the Roses and the English Civil War, armies have fought in – and over – Yorkshire.

And today it is home to army garrisons, air force bases and military training camps. Catterick, three miles south of Richmond, is the British Army's biggest military garrison.

It is also the spiritual home of Military Spirit Gin, for it was here the gin's co-founders first met as they completed their basic army training.

Claire Norton and Pete Griffiths have created a complex artisan gin based around botanicals that have both historical and current military connotations.

Lime flowers were used to calm soldiers during the Second World War, while yarrow once regularly saw service to stem the flow of blood and was often known as soldier's woundwort. Another old battlefield medicine is broadleaf plantain which was known as the soldier's herb.

Many modern soldiers will associate gorse with Britain's military training grounds, while both hawthorn berries and heather flowers symbolise protection and red clover flowers are for health and good fortune.

Distiller, Tony Brotherton, a fellow army veteran, uses these botanicals alongside juniper to create the Military Spirit signature gin at the Yorkshire Dales Distillery at Colburn near the Catterick Garrison.

With all those military connections, the gin appropriately supports SSAFA, the charity which provides lifelong support to the armed forces, veterans and their families.

For Claire, creating a London Dry gin was the obvious next step, having bought the Ripon-based Little Red Berry Co in 2017. Founded by Rachel Jamieson in 2011, the Little Red Berry Co produces alcoholic liqueurs and favoured gins using fruit from Yorkshire farms.

Its drinks are handmade by maturing the fruit and sugar in a spirit and the gin-based liqueurs include damson and raspberry. There's also Lemon & Thyme or Elderflower & Cucumber flavoured gins.

MOLOTOV GIN

Leeds, West Yorkshire
www.molotovgin.com
Launched: August 2018

If you want to get people to drink your gin you need to attract their attention. No better way than with an eye-catching name – especially one that has an explosive connotation.

Vyacheslav Mikhailovich Molotov was an influential Soviet politician in the period before the Second World War. As Soviet foreign minister, he was one of the architects of the Molotov-Ribbentrop Pact which agreed that Nazi Germany would not intervene in the Soviet war against Finland.

As they fought back, the Finns called the hand-held bottle firebombs developed to attack Soviet tanks "Molotov cocktails".

When Dayle Roane decided to create a gin, he wanted to capture an explosion of flavour which would be great neat or over ice and be strong enough to "boss the tonic".

Dayle, who had worked in the international banking environment, had become enthralled with gin in the 1990s when he was entertaining clients in London. At that time, the gin on offer was limited – and no-one even thought of sipping gin neat.

In the new millennium, with the liberation of the spirits industry in the UK and the growth of craft distilling, the style of drinking gin had changed. And Dayle started to dream of creating a gin which would stand tall and be appreciated by gin lovers.

He worked with a gin adviser, the master distiller David T Smith, for nine months to create the Molotov recipe. After ten distillations they had found the perfect blend for their 12 botanicals – juniper, wormwood, Seville orange, fennel, angelica, red peppercorns, grapefruit, lemongrass, coriander,

112 ·   YORKSHIRE'S GINS

makrut lime leaves, ginger and nutmeg.

The complex London Dry gin is all Dayle hoped for: from its juniper-forward notes, through the refreshing citrus flavours to the spicy warmth.

Now, Dayle has big aspirations for his company, Molotov Brand, and he wants it to become known internationally for creating premium, complex and beautifully nuanced spirits that deliver a true taste experience.

OH MY GIN 45%

Harden, West Yorkshire
www.ohmygin45.com
Launched: January 2017

Oh My Gin 45% is the creation of a gin-loving former professional golfer. Ian Bottomley had been working in the brewing industry since putting away his clubs after stints as a club professional in both Yorkshire and Germany and two years on the European Challenge Tour having represented England as a schoolboy.

In the 1980s when gin was not as trendy as it is today, pink gins made with Angostura Bitters and G&Ts were the drinks of choice in many golf clubs. It was there that Ian got a taste for gin.

Over the years he enjoyed dry martinis (made with gin, of course) with his friend Rick Glover and his wife Judith. When they both died of cancer, Ian realised his fascination for gin could be put to good use and decided to make a gin in their honour. The eternal knot and black lines on the label are in their memory.

He went to Charles Maxwell at the Thames Distillery to create a London Dry Gin with a "strong backbone and rounded character that brings plenty to the table at parties", just like the Glovers.

OMG45% is juniper heavy, with orange and lemon for citrus notes alongside warmth from coriander and cinnamon. Ian was determined it should make a great dry martini – one that "slides down the gullet like the devil in velvet trousers", as Rick would have described it.

In the summer of July 2019, Ian added six flavoured gins to his portfolio. Using the 45% ABV signature gin as a base, the flavours – Passion Fruit, Clementine, Pink Grapefruit, Blueberry, Rhubarb and Scottish Raspberry – are added post-distillation.

So, what's next for the Bingley-born businessman? He's preparing to become a distiller himself, with studying and red tape to navigate en route to setting up his own distillery.

PHURE GIN

Brighouse, West Yorkshire and Conway, Wales
www.phure-liquors.com
Launched: December 2015

When three chemists decided to make gin, it was inevitable they would approach it in a scientific manner.

Andy Whiting, Euan Noble and Kevin Flower used their expertise in chemistry to think about ways that they might be able to extract and distil botanicals to create a unique product.

Their solution was to develop a low-temperature extraction process followed by a low pressure/low temperature distillation through glass.

With the three friends based in Yorkshire, Durham and Conway, the midpoint of the experimentation was Brighouse, where Euan owns a bar and the Rokt Activity Centre at the former Sugden's flour mill.

The resulting pHure Gin – made with juniper and eight other botanicals, including coriander, cardamom, fennel and citrus – debuted at the Millers Bar, and it gained popularity steadily in the area.

However, a flood in Brighouse and the purchase of larger equipment meant they decided to relocate the distilling to Conway where Kevin, the production director, is based and uses the new glass vacuum distillation still.

PHure is now as much a Welsh as a Yorkshire product, with bi-lingual labels and a flagship pHure Conway Gin.

There is now a vodka alongside seasonal flavoured gins, including an autumnal blackberry and apple edition launched in October 2019.

With the distance between Wales and Brighouse, it is good to note that the three scientists have factored their environmental impact into their equations.

Not only does their low-temperature gin making use less power than traditional methods, they have installed solar panels which generate twice what they need in power, they use sustainably-sourced ingredients and they recycle and compost wherever possible.

RHUBARB TRIANGLE GIN

That Boutique-y Gin Company, Kent
www.thatboutiqueygincompany.com
Launched: November 2017

That Boutique-y Gin Company is well known for its quirky take on things. As a result it has an innovative portfolio of gins introducing flavours such as Yuzo, Neroli, Smoked Rosemary and Cucamelon.

Over the years, That Boutique-y Gin Co's approach has morphed from "why not?" into "because we can". It is part of Atom Group, which was started in a tin shed by a group of childhood friends who shared a love of spirits and now includes Bathtub Gin and the Master of Malt online retailer.

When it came to creating a rhubarb gin, there was only one place for That Boutique-y Gin Co to source the hero ingredient – Yorkshire's Rhubarb Triangle. The nine-square-mile area between Leeds, Bradford and Wakefield has been specialising in the pink-stalked vegetable since the 1870s and, since 2010, Yorkshire forced rhubarb has had Protected Designation of Origin (PDO) status.

The juice used in Rhubarb Triangle Gin comes from plants cultivated within the PDO area. The rhubarb is grown outdoors where the sunlight produces a tarter, bolder character than the indoors-grown forced crop. The fresh juice is combined with sugar and a gin which features orange, lemon, nutmeg, cassia, cinnamon, orris, liquorice, coriander seed, angelica and juniper.

The label – designed by That Boutique-y's resident food and drink illustrator Grace J Ward from Hertfordshire – subtly incorporates the outlines of the coats of arms of the triangle's three cities in the rhubarb leaves which sit on juniper berries.

SKOSH SMOKED
& SPICED DRY GIN

Micklegate, York
skoshyork.co.uk
Launched: December 2018

Small plates of refined Asian-inspired cuisine are the signature of York chef Neil Bentinck.

His restaurant Skosh, meaning "small amount" in Japanese, has been exciting diners since 2016 with these inventive culinary morsels.

They are influenced by Neil's Indian family heritage and his travels around the world. He incorporates a range of flavours from across Asia – from the Middle East through to Japan – using Yorkshire and British produce.

The menu is eclectic with some quite exotic food combinations, and it has attracted glowing reviews and plenty of awards.

When Neil wanted a craft gin to compliment his menu, he turned to the Cooper King Distillery at Sutton-on-the-Forest which had just gone into production.

He worked with co-founders Abbie Neilson and Chris Jaume to capture his vision of including full-on flavours in his gin. The result is that black cardamom, nori, mandarin and Szechuan peppercorn are skilfully layered to create a complex and full-bodied spirit.

Skosh Smoked + Spiced Dry Gin is hand distilled, bottled and labelled at Cooper King and which, as befits its sustainable approach to distilling, makes good use of resources, for instance using renewable energy.

The approach continues with Skosh Gin, where when only the husks of the key smoked cardamom are required, the hearts are used in one of the distillery's own Pilot Series spirits.

SLINGSBY GIN

Harrogate, North Yorkshire
wslingsby.co.uk
Launched: September 2015

Taking the waters was what made Harrogate famous. Today, another liquid is putting the elegant spa town in the headlines – and it's gin.

Slingsby Gin has captured the glamour of the town's history and become the foundation of a modern landmark – the Spirit of Harrogate on Montpellier Parade.

The gin is named after the man who discovered the water which was to fuel Harrogate's growth.

The town sits on an underground aquifer fed by water off the moors and woodlands and filtered slowly through layers of rock.

Although there are said to be 88 mineral springs in the area, it was the discovery of Tewit Well on the Stray in the late 16th century by William Slingsby that gave birth to the town's spa culture.

In the following years, wealthy visitors flocked there to take the mineral waters for the benefit of their health, putting Harrogate firmly on the map. Inspired by this story, Marcus Black and Mike Carthy set about creating a drink that would capture Harrogate's heritage and reflect the essence of the modern-day town.

The pair, who own Intercontinental Brands, a specialist drinks company, took 15 months to develop the gin – considering 18 recipes before they found the one which became Slingsby London Dry Gin.

It uses 24 botanicals, 12 of which are from the kitchen garden on the Rudding Park estate and five from further afield in Yorkshire.

To reflect the restorative nature of Harrogate, there is primrose, sweet cicely, nettle, rhubarb, milk thistle, rosehip and Taylors of Harrogate green and jasmine tea. The gin's citrus note comes from grapefruit.

The botanicals are sent to Langley Distillery in the Midlands where they are macerated with English wheat spirit for 12 hours. The spirit is then distilled in Jenny, a 10,000-litre still. Dilution with Harrogate's spring water is done at Slingsby's production facilities in Middlesbrough.

Slingsby Yorkshire Rhubarb Gin followed, infusing the signature London Dry Gin with rhubarb from E Oldroyd & Sons at Rothwell in the Yorkshire Triangle.

Joining the line-up of bold square bottles are Navy Strength, Old Tom and Gooseberry gins, as well as a limited edition Marmalade Gin … and vodka.

Not content with creating distinctive gins, the Slingsby team has launched Solo, a range of ready-to-serve G&Ts, worked with a Michelin-starred chef … and Carthy & Black, a cream and Slingsby Gin liqueur, is on the market.

Slingsby shares its spiritual home with the public at the Spirit of Harrogate. Close to the landmark Bettys Café Tea Rooms, it is both a shop and place to explore and enjoy gin and is becoming a tourist destination in its own right.

TAILORS GIN

Grand Arcade, Leeds
www.TailorsGin.com
Launched: August 2018

Yorkshire is recognised for many things including its textiles, and Leeds developed a reputation as a centre for using the cloth made in the area. This tradition of tailoring lives on in the city today. Not surprising then that there is a gin which celebrates its craft.

Tailors Gin is the creation of Matt Wignall, a tailor, and Jamila Juma-Ware, an events and marketing director.

The Gentleman's Tailor, as Matt is known, travels across the north of England making bespoke suits, shirts and overcoats, using the finest cloth, much of it made in Yorkshire.

He can also be found under the ornate arches of the Grand Arcade in Leeds, in a quintessentially British tailor's shop.

In the evenings at the weekends, the shop transforms into a gin lounge revelling in the atmosphere of the "roaring" 1920s.

Matt and Jamila teamed up to create a gin which would be the perfect fit for the bar where guests can borrow vintage costumes and strike a pose in the art deco interior or beside up-cycled sewing tables.

Their small batch gin has been fashioned with a made-to-measure selection of British botanicals. Using juniper, coriander, mint, cardamom, angelica, chamomile, lemon peel and bergamot, the London Dry-style gin is made for them in Staffordshire.

Tailors' vintage-style ceramic bottles give the gin an intriguing period look.

A sister brand Drapers is measuring up for release in the future.

ZACHARIAH STORM GIN

Robin Hood's Bay, North Yorkshire
baytownrhb.com
Launched: October 2015

Smuggling was almost a way of life in parts of Yorkshire's east coast. Villages tucked into the folds of the cliffs were the gateway for contraband which had come across the North Sea. Celebrating this history of Robin Hood's Bay is a collection of spirits from Baytown, which also has a range of smugglers' beers.

The spirits commemorate the characters who inhabited the maze of streets and secret passageways in Robin Hood's Bay – or Baytown as it is also known.

Zachariah Storm Gin was devised by Paul Johnston who was then the managing director of Baytown, and it is made by Raisthorpe Manor in Wharram. It is likely that members of a village family called Storm would have been involved in the smuggling trade.

Alongside the gin is a whisky honouring the 21st Light Dragoon, the soldiers who patrolled the coastal areas to apprehend the smuggling gangs. There is also Squire Farsyde Port which reminds us that it was not only the village folk who were involved in smuggling. In Fylingthorpe, at Thorpe Hall, the squire's home in those wild days, there is a secret stone hide thought to have been used to stash contraband.

Finally, there is Lingers' Ghost Vodka. Legend says that a rider in white, mounted on a white horse would be seen at Lingers' Hill on the edge of Baytown before a smuggling run took place.

Featuring the illustrations of Shropshire book jacket illustrator Chris Brown, the bottle labels were designed by Hutton Peach in York to capture the spirit of characters of the smuggling era.

Baytown Beers is now owned by Brenda and Steve Smith who also have the Station Road Stores & Post Office in Robin Hood's Bay.

SPIRITS OF MYSTERY

Most people are happy to tell the world about their gin, but there are a few in Yorkshire who seem reluctant to shout about their product. I've tried very hard to find out about every gin on the market in Yorkshire so that this is a truly comprehensive guide. However, a few did not respond and they remain a mystery. In addition, some gins are no longer in production, and there are a couple who didn't want to be included because their plans were "up in the air".

The shy "mystery" gins are often in the marketplace – you'll see them at farmers' markets, independent shops, gin festivals and in bars but usually on a small scale. And, as is the way of the web, you will find them on the internet. So, for the sake of completeness, here are the gins that I found in Yorkshire, but could not include as complete profiles.

Brittains Gin – a Doncaster-based vodka company also has a range of gins presented with a flamingo on the bottle

Cottingley Fairytale Gins – often on sale in York's Shambles market celebrating the fairies of the West Yorkshire village

Drunken Cow – launched in the summer of 2019 for the Crown Inn at Hawes in Wensleydale

Fourfolk Gin – created by two brothers and their wives in Haworth and sold at markets in the area

Issac Poad – a North Yorkshire brewer with a strong heritage in brewing and malting has had a London Dry Gin on the market since 2017

Royal Spring's Three Sisters Gin – one from West Yorkshire to keep an eye on

Sacred Bat Gin – a crowdfunded gin on the east coast which seems not to have progressed to reality

Spirits of Bronte's Yorkshire Lass Gin – no longer in production

Tykes Gin – a strawberry gin launched in the summer of 2019 using real strawberries.

TONIC WATER

There are few things in life which go together better than gin and tonic. Few of us can resist a G&T – if it's not the epitome of a summer Saturday, I don't know what is. In recent years things have changed: gone is the obligatory G& "Schhh, you know who" – today it's all about complementing the flavours of each gin's botanicals.

In Yorkshire, it is distillers themselves who have been leading the way in creating tonics for the craft gins reaching the market.

Admittedly, in the UK the biggest independent names are Fentimans of Northumberland, Fever Tree of Somerset and Franklin & Sons of London, but Yorkshire companies are making a stand. Here, we look at two tonic waters made in Yorkshire.

GASCOIGNE'S

West Yorkshire
haworthsteambrewery.co.uk
Launched: March 2018
Andy Gascoigne started making gin at Haworth Steam Brewery in 2017 and he soon realised it needed some perfect partners: small-batch all-natural tonics and mixers.

His aim was to create drinks that were both perfect for pairing with the finest spirits and a refreshing drink in their own right – all made in Yorkshire.

The resulting Gascoigne's Tonics & Mixers use fresh ingredients from pressed fruits, sourced where possible from British growers, with no artificial colouring or sweeteners.

The tonics use natural quinine and the range includes Pomegranate, Marmalade, English Cucumber, Lemon Twist and Red Gooseberry. The mixers include Rhubarb & Ginger, Blackcurrant & Liquorice, Strawberry & Vanilla Sours and Sour Bramley Apple.

Andy, a brewer and distiller, already had experience he could call on for the venture. He had honed his carbonation techniques a decade or so earlier when he started to bottle the beer he was making at the Oyster Brewery Bar & Restaurant on the remote Isle of Seil on Scotland's West Coast.

Back home in West Yorkshire, Andy started making his tonics at a site in Cleckheaton but quickly outgrew the space and the production facilities will be in a new home soon.

In a neat quirk, that original Gascoigne production line was in the town where George Fentiman started making botanically brewed ginger beer in 1905. From that enterprise grew one of the UK's leading tonic brands.

RAISTHORPE

Wharram, North Yorkshire
www.raisthorpemanor.com
Launched: 2018

Raisthorpe Manor Fine Foods already had a decade of experience making fruit liqueurs, vodka, jams and gin when it launched its range of tonics.

Its founder Julia Medforth decided to celebrate the company's tenth anniversary with a perfect partner for gin.

It took about six months to develop Raisthorpe Yorkshire Tonic Waters, with the time spent choosing ingredients and blending botanicals to make sure the balance of flavours was just right.

Made and bottled at the company's Thixendale site close to its Wharram home in the Yorkshire Wolds, Raisthorpe's tonics are unique in that they contain only natural ingredients and Vitamin C.

As an alternative to quinine, they use the South American botanical quassia which has no bitter aftertaste.

The water comes from the underwater streams of the Gypsey Race on the Yorkshire Wolds. The Gypsey Race, which rises close to Wharram, flows underground through clarifying chalk before it resurfaces and continues east towards the North Sea.

Legend has it that when the Gypsey Race is in flood, bad things happen, with the Great Plague, restoration of Charles II and William of Orange's accession being credited to its prophetic powers.

The Raisthorpe Yorkshire Tonic range includes Premium Tonic Water, Citrus, Strawberry & Pomegranate, Pink Grapefruit, Apple & Elderflower and Skinny Tonic.

AUTHOR'S THANKS

Gin has become quite an adventure for me, and a lot of people have supported me as the brilliant wheeze of writing about gin has grown into a serious research project. My friends have humoured my fascination for bottle design, attending gin events, and happily helped with a bit of tasting. The fact I'm now on to my second book is testament to that support.

Across the Yorkshire gin community I have had enormous support – the distillers, makers, owners, ambassadors and experts of every sort have been incredibly generous with their time. I won't single anyone out as that would be unfair, but I hope this book will repay their investment in me.

At Great Northern Books, David Burrill has come up with the striking cover for this book. I adore the way he has been inspired by Yorkshire's stunning landscapes and has moved the design on from his clever take on Charles Rennie Mackintosh which graced The GIN CLAN's cover.

This has been a personal trip into my past. My mother's family was from Leeds and I spent a good deal of my childhood in Yorkshire, living there for five years, so it has been such fun to use gin to reacquaint myself with those roots.

The first person I ever saw drinking gin and tonic would have been my mother. Long, with lots of ice and lemon – and made by my father. Not drunk often, but just at the times when it was the perfect thing to drink. Gin was obviously not mother's ruin because, right up to two weeks before she died at the age of 96 in December 2019, my mother was proofreading this book. Thank you!

Fiona Laing

Edinburgh, January 2020

INDEX

Gins, makers and distilleries in the Clan and Kith & Kin listings

Artful Pour 86

Assay 54

Bar Walls 87

Barghest 74

Barnsley Dry 70

Barnsley Hospice 72

Beerhouses 33

Beverley 88

Black Sheep 91

Brittains 121

Campbell's of Leyburn 92

Captain Cook
Distillery 14

Cardamom 28

Cartwright & Butler
Darjeeling Infused 94

Chocolate Malt Barley 64

Citra 33

Cooper King Distillery 16

Cottingley Fairytale ... 121

Dandelion & Burdock . 73

Deckchair 24

Desert Ram 82

Divine 48

Double Sloe Gin 79

Downtown Abbey 95

Drapers 118

Drunken Cow 121

Elderflower Orchard 69

English Cassis Gin 79

Evil Eye 97

Father of All Evil 97

Folklore Society 99

Forest Fruits Gin 20

Forged in Wakefield 18

Fourfolk 121

Ginger Ninja 36

Granny Garbutt's 100

Greystone 102

Harbinger 36

Harewood 102

Harrison Distillery 20

Harrogate Gin 22

Harrogate Tipple 22

Haworth Steam
Brewing Co 24

Hedgerow 60

Hedgerow Pink 66

Herb Gin 16

Honeyberry 44

Hooting Owl Distillery 26

Hotham's Distillery 28

Hull Dry 30

Humber Street
Distillery 30

Issac Poad 121

JacqSon 32

JP Adlam 34

King Billy 104

Kingtree 42

Kure 36

Lamplighter 24

Leeds 105

Lickerish Tooth
Distillery 36

Locksley Distilling Co 38

Man Behind the
Curtain 106

Marmalade 70

Masala Chai 64

Masons Distillery 40

Midsummer Nights ... 107

Military Spirit 108

Mill House Distillery .. 42

Miss Mollies 24

Molotov 110

Moorland 66

Mother of All Evil 97

Navigator: First Voyage 14

Northern Fox Distillery 44

Num8er Eorl Crabtree 49

Oh My Gin 45% 112

Outlaw 80

Peach Perfect 69

pHure Liquors 113

Pink Particular 78

Pride in Hull 28

Priory Farm 46

Purple Ram 82

R2 Distillers 48

Raisthorpe Manor 50

Rare Bird Distillery 52

Rhubarb Triangle 114

Ripon Cathedral
St Wilfrid's 41

Roman Fruit 80

Royal Fox 20

Royal Spring 121

Sacred Bat 121

Sheep's Eye 36

Sheffield Distillery 54

Sheffield Dry 70

Shibden Valley 62

Shiny Cowbird
Spirit Co........................ 56

Sing Gin 58

Sir Robin of Locksley... 38

Skosh Smoked
& Spiced 115

Slingsby 116

Sloemotion 60

SP8 62

Speight's 62

Spirit of Harrogate 116

Spirit of Masham
Distillery 64

Spirit of Swaledale 66

Spirits of Bronte 121

Spitfire 24

Stoker 74

Summer Solstice 78

Summertide 17

Tailors 118

Taplin & Mageean
Spirit Co 68

Three Sisters 122

Trawler 30

True North Brew Co ... 70

Tykes 121

VIE Spirited 26

Viola Old Tom 28

VSOT 38

Waterton's Reserve 72

Wensleydale Dry 68

Wensleydale Heifer 50

West Riding Distillery . 72

Whitby Distillery 74

White House Distillery 76

Whittaker's Distillery ... 78

Wild Old Tom 74

Wild Ram 82

Wild Winter Berry 107

Winter Solstice 78

YD 82

York Gin Co................. 80

Yorkshire Dales
Distillery....................... 82

Yorkshire Lass 121

Zachariah Storm 120

Also available from Great Northern Books

The Gin Clan
by Fiona Laing

Scotland's gin scene is thriving: a clan of distillers is creating passionately conceived and beautifully crafted gins, using the finest locally sourced ingredients. We tell the stories of the spirits, where Scotland's gin industry has come from and where it's going.

Gins from crofts, towns, herb gardens and even an old vet school – we list not just Scotland's signature gins but all the distilleries that make them.

www.gnbooks.co.uk